£2-00

NORTHERN INDIA

NEPAL • BHUTAN

Corinne Bloch

GW00467926

JPMGUIDES

CONTENTS

many faiths

palatial architecture

stunning smiles and colours

local transport

THIS WAY NORTHERN INDIA

To anyone with a spirit of adventure, India presents a superb challenge. It never leaves you indifferent. Its magic lies in the sheer profusion of peoples and landscapes enclosed within this diamond-shaped sub-continent, extending over 3,000 km (1,865 miles) from the northern mountains of Kashmir to the southernmost tip of Cape Comorin on the Indian Ocean.

East to west, it stretches another 3,000 km from the border with China and Myanmar (Burma) to the Gujarat coast on the Arabian Sea. If superimposed on Europe, it would reach from Sicily to the North Cape.

The bare statistics are enough to make your head spin. By 2025, India—the largest democracy on earth—will have overtaken China as the world's most populous country. People are everywhere, crowding each other into the roadway, bulging out of auto-rickshaws, perching on roofs of buses and trains, loading a family of four onto a single motor scooter. The ethnic diversity is there to see on a rupee banknote where the amount is printed in most of the 22 state-recognized languages, in addition to English. Linguists have counted over 400 dialects actually being spoken all over the country, using 13 different alphabets. Hindi is the most-spoken language, but not by the majority of the population. English, which has the status of subsidiary official language, is spoken by only 3 per cent of the people, most of them in the big cities.

Land of Paradox

Perhaps because of this extraordinary mix of cultures, the modern country soars from one extreme to the other. The cradle of non-violence, it is restless, turbulent, passionate, exhilarating, infuriating. Still 70 per cent rural, India has 400 million destitute people living on its streets, yet there will be no fewer than 400,000 dollar-millionaires by 2015. While real estate in cities such as Mumbai is among the most expensive in the world, the Indian peninsula also harbours the largest shanty towns of Asia.

In a few years from now, land for construction will be at such a premium that even the tiniest patch belonging to the poorest family will be worth a fortune.

With all the fervour and conviction of days gone by, India still cremates its dead on the banks of the Ganges. Half-naked *sadhu*—ascetics depending entirely on charity—pursue their quest for spirituality and redemption, rarely speaking unless they are reciting their prayers. Meanwhile in Bangalore, Mumbai and New Delhi, young Hindus in jeans and trainers write computer software for American clients and continually re-invent the world of information technology, discussing the terms of their contracts in a polished English that would not be out of place at an Oxford high table.

Anchored in Tradition

Northern India is all the richer in customs and architectural styles because it was more frequently the target of Central Asian and European invaders than the southern part of the country. After the Aryans, the Persians, the Scythians and the Huns, the Moghuls left the palaces you see when you travel from the green plains of Madhya Pradesh to the Rajasthan desert.

Further reminders of this turbulent past are the incongruous Victorian monuments that were bequeathed by the Raj. Today, the entire Western world, under the guise of progress and modernity, is gradually being assimilated into Indian society.

This capacity to absorb new ideas, whether cultural, economic or religious, without weakening in the slightest their respect for ancestral traditions, has been the greatest strength of the Indian people for more than 3,000 years. As a result, India's culture is one of the most long-lived and fascinating in existence. Neither the influence of the Aryans nor even that of the Muslims has managed to put an end to customs perpetuated since the dawn of time. Indeed, the origins of Ayurvedic medicine, revived and practised worldwide in this "New Age", of vegetarianism, of the mother-goddess and the great god Shiva, date back to long before the first invasions and trace their roots to the primitive tribes of the subcontinent.

Strong Faith

At the beginning of the 21st century, India's religions enjoy a healthy following that astonishes the Western world. The country has welcomed industrialization with open arms. It may train 600,000 engineers and 300,000 technicians every year on its university benches, boast experts in information technology and send satellites into space, but nothing seems to dent the power of the Hindu pantheon. It will take more than a few nuclear tests to make Shiva tremble, and more than contact with IBM or Microsoft to westernize Vishnu.

Democratic Revolution

Since the proclamation of Independence in 1947, the nation has been a democracy; it seems to have successfully adopted a political system that was, at the outset, ill-suited to its diverse population and internal tensions. From one election to the next—and there have been many since the leading parties proved unable to obtain an overall majority—the people are demonstrating more and more their commitment to democratic government.

However, it was not until the 1980s that a proper democratic revolution took place, important enough to transform the political landscape and diminish the historic Congress Party to the advantage of the right-wing Hindu nationalists—though the situation was reversed in 2004. Steps taken towards economic liberalization in 1991, sweeping away part of the legislative and trade barriers and opening the market to foreign investors, also favoured the emergence of a new force—300 million consumers.

Huber/Picture Finders

Even the elephants are allowed to wear makeup.

For several years now, the country has revolved around this rising middle class, whose increasing power is shaking the foundations of the caste system by bringing to the fore people from the lower levels of society. The arrival of this new class is disrupting the established social order and exacerbating fundamentalism.

From behind her shimmering veil of traditions, Mother India is watching over a country that is strongly committed to improving its economic growth.

A place of legend, like most temples in India, Chaturbhuj Mandir in Orchha.

Carol Mitchell

FLASHBACK

From meagre fossil remains, it can be assumed that the Indian subcontinent was inhabited by *Homo erectus* 50,000 years ago. At the end of the last Ice Age, about 12,000 years ago, neolithic populations began to occupy the region. The shelters of Bhimbetka in Madhya Pradesh, a UNESCO World Heritage site, are decorated with prized petroglyphs and prehistoric paintings.

From about 3300 BC to 1900 BC, one of the most refined cultures of the ancient world settled in the Indus Basin (present-day Pakistan), spreading over a territory that covered the Punjab, Rajasthan and Gujarat. The existence of this so-called "Indus civilization", with links to the Sumerians, was revealed at the end of the 19th century, when the ruins of their cities were excavated from a blanket of sand. The modernity of their achievements—houses with several storeys, bathrooms, sewers, planned streets, jewellery and a written language—indicates an evolved culture that has reached its zenith. However, there are few clues to help trace its development, and its script has still not been deciphered.

Indo-Aryan Invasions

The prevailing theory, now increasingly challenged, suggests that at the end of the Bronze Age, around 1700–1500 BC, nomadic Indo-Aryan peoples, perhaps originating in Russia and Central Asia, migrated to present-day Iran and from there to Northern India. They intermixed with the populations of the Indus and imposed new political, religious and social structures of an Indo-European type. They were thought to be at the origin of the difference between northern and southern India, where the dark-skinned Dravidian inhabitants are predominantly vegetarian, having escaped Aryan occupation.

Religious Evolution

If this invasion theory is to be believed, the Indo-Aryan conquerors reduced the Dravidians to slavery and imposed the caste system that still dominates today, while assimilating customs and divinities, giving rise to a reli-

Devanagari ("city of the gods") script is used for Sanskrit and Hindi.

gious syncretism at the origin of the Hindu religion. However, Indian archaeologists tend to favour the hypothesis of a much earlier division of India, with the Dravidian peoples of the south migrating much earlier, and those of the north descending from the Indus civilization. It would seem that the roots of Hinduism are to be found here, among these peaceful peoples who succumbed to prolonged drought rather than to massive invasion. To back up this version, no traces of destruction have been excavated. Perhaps the truth lies in a compromise: it is easy to imagine a strong link between the Indus and Hinduism, without rejecting the hypothesis of population movements from present-day Iran.

Appearance of Sanskrit

In this complicated melting pot, before the first millennium BC, the main vehicle of the Indian civilization, the Sanskrit language, took shape. Hindi, the official language of the country today, derived from it, as well as most of the idioms now used in the north of the peninsula. The sacred texts of Hinduism, the books of the *Veda*, were written in Sanskrit in around 1000 BC. Sanskrit is thus the most ancient of the Indo-European languages of which spoken forms still survive. Greek, Latin, Persian and the Germanic and Celtic languages all belong to the same linguistic family.

Perhaps influenced by the traditional pastoralism of the Indo-Aryan peoples, the Vedas made the cow sacred. The epic of the *Mahabharata* was created, before that of the *Ramayana*. Society underwent a transformation, agriculture was developed and the first kingdoms and city-states of the Mahajanapada emerged. Buddhism and Jainism expanded after 500 BC, along with yoga and the concept of reincarnation.

First Empires

The kings of Persia, followed by Alexander the Great, reached the subcontinent but never succeeded in settling there. Originating in the eastern plain of the Ganges at the beginning of the 4th century BC, the Mauryan empire rapidly spread with the victories of Ashoka the Great (c. 269–232 BC). Soon covering 5 million sq km, it included almost all of the Indian subcontinent, Pakistan, Afghanistan, the eastern part of Iran and the land stretching eastwards to Assam. Buddhism rose to be the state religion, and art and culture flourished. (The modern State of India has taken the lion motif of Ashoka's Pillar as its emblem, see pp. 14, 89.) The Mauryan empire dissolved in the 2nd century BC. The subcontinent broke up into competing kingdoms and empires with ever-changing boundaries. Commerce with Rome began, via Egypt. In the 4th century, the Gupta dynasty succeeded in unifying the North. A new golden age favoured the development of the arts and sciences; the decimal system was devised, and the concept of zero. The Hindu culture took form while Buddhism gradually dwindled in importance after the 8th century.

Rajput Clans

The Rajputs strengthened their power in the northwest of the country from the 4th century onwards. They remained part of the political scene first under Muslim domination and later under the British. Their heirs, the maharajahs, even managed to retain their privileges until the middle of the 20th century. Their forefathers may have been of Indian origin or were perhaps Huns who arrived here in the 5th century. The Rajputs themselves blithely created their own mythical genealogy, claiming direct descent from the brother of the god Rama. Being of low birth they were thus able to filter into the warrior caste, the *kshatriya*.

Subsequently, history and legend blended so well, and the Rajputs' chivalrous spirit earned them so much glory, that numerous other dynasties of far more noble lineage falsified their own genealogy to lay claim to Rajput ancestry. Divided into several clans, the great feudal Rajputs shared the region until the 12th century, in an uneasy alliance marked by bitter internal strife.

Muslim Invasion

The Arabian peninsula was not unknown to the ancient Indians, and the city of Mahesvara—identified with Mecca—is mentioned as one of the sacred places of the cult of Shiva. The birth of the Prophet Muhammad in 570 and the subsequent birth of Islam were destined to overturn the world.

Muslims settled in the Indus valley in the 8th century, then in Afghanistan. From there they launched their first incursions into northern India, destroying holy places and sacking the city of Varanasi. But it would not be until the end of the 12th century that Muhammad of Ghor, an Afghan prince, took Rajasthan, then Delhi, Varanasi and the whole of the Ganges valley. From then on, the emerging empire never stopped expanding until its fall more than five centuries later.

A slave by the name of Qutb-ud-Din, general and successor of Muhammad, founded the Sultanate of Delhi in 1206; he became the first independent Muslim emperor of India. The "Slave Dynasty" (Mamelukes) reigned until 1290, preceding four other Muslim dynasties which remained in power till the arrival of the Moghuls in 1526. Delhi was sacked by the armies of Tamerlaine (Timur) in 1398, 100,000 prisoners of war were executed.

Cohabitation With the Hindus

The Muslims never allowed themselves to be absorbed by Hinduism, nor did they succeed in imposing their own religion. Even today, despite the exchange of populations after the partition of India and Pakistan in 1947, they represent 13.4 per cent of the inhabitants of India. The conflicts that still govern relations between the communities dates in fact from the days of Qutb-ud-Din.

The large number of Rajput clans made it impossible for the Sultanate to bring all the regions under submission. Confrontations are incessant, despite some necessary attempts at collaboration, as witnessed by the emergence at this time of a common language, Urdu. A combination of Persian vocabulary and Hindu grammar, it remains the everyday language of Pakistan and is still spoken in northern India.

Moghul Era

Babar or Babur, descendant of Tamerlane and the Mongol leader Ghengis Khan, reigned over a small kingdom in Central Asia. In 1526, he overthrew the Sultanate of Delhi and founded the Moghul Empire on its ruins. (The word *Moghul* is the Persian translation of Mongol.) "Hindustan," he wrote, "is a country which reveals very few attractive facets. The inhabitants (…) are without intelligence and coarse (…). They build without concern for beauty or elegance." Babar was destined to have a great influence on Indian architecture, and during the Moghul era monuments as magnificent as the Taj Mahal were built.

Babar was succeeded by his son Humayun, but the empire's most fascinating personality is without doubt his grandson, Emperor Akbar, who reigned from 1556 until 1605. Under his rule, all religions were tolerated, and he even invented his own, which died with him. He abolished the taxes imposed on non-Muslims and, following a policy begun by his predecessors to consolidate the empire, initiated a process of conciliation towards the Rajputs by naming them heads of his armies and by marrying several Rajput princesses. Indeed, certain Rajasthani families owe to Akbar the prestige they still enjoy today.

Akbar's successors were not all as enlightened nor as tolerant. Fresh conflicts with the Rajputs, Persian incursions and the rise of the Marathas (a confederation of small Hindu kingdoms in central India) caused the disintegration of the empire—given the final blow by the British who arrived on the subcontinent in 1803.

Europeans Enter the Scene

Portuguese navigator Vasco da Gama was the first European to accost the Malabar Coast in the southwest, arriving in 1498. The Portuguese were also the last to leave India, not relinquishing their colonies of Damman, Diu and Goa until 1961.

The ships of the new English East India Company debarked in Surat in 1608, after an agreement signed with the Moghul emperor, while the Dutch settled in Ceylon (1640) and on the Malabar coast after chasing out the Portuguese. Some time later, the French established settlements at Chandernagor (1673) and Pondichéry

commons.wikimedia.org

Emperor Akbar hunting with cheetahs, from the *Akbar Nama* (1602).

(1674). But by then, the British had already set up posts in Madras, Calcutta and Bombay.

Anglo-French Conflict

During the 18th century, things began to warm up as the colonial ambitions of the British started to overtake their commercial objectives. The control of trade with India became the prize during a century of conflict with the French, a situation which was to have its repercussions on the conflicts between local empires. The English East India Company played the Rajputs off against the Marathas, the latter being supported by France. In 1803, its armies captured Delhi from the Marathas. Gradually, all of India fell into British hands. Only Nepal, in exchange for a few provinces, would never become a possession of the Company.

Indian Mutiny

India remained an aggregate of states, many of which enjoyed only the appearance of independence. In reality, the new masters imposed their administration on the small states, putting forward the poor management of business as their reason. Despoiled by the great landowners, thousands of families were reduced to a state of poverty. By virtue of treaties signed with the British, even the Rajput princes were subdued, though they were not totally deprived of authority for the British wanted to ensure their support in case of insurrection— something which did eventually happen in 1857.

The affair that shook the country was unfairly perceived as a British lack of sensitivity for the local culture. The sepoys, Indian soldiers in the service of the Crown, were told to bite open their cartridges before inserting them into the rifle breech. But rumours led the Hindus to believe that the cartridges were greased with tallow, from the sacred cow, while the Muslims suspected it was lard, from the unclean pig. (It was, in fact, a mixture of linseed oil and beeswax.) The sepoys triggered off a mutiny that spread all over northern India.

Imperial Years

The rebellion was put down with the help of the Rajput princes. The British Crown took over the power hitherto wielded by the East India Company, and in Delhi Queen Victoria was proclaimed Empress of India on January 1, 1877. Two kinds of territories were defined: British India, ruled directly by the colonial government, and the Native States placed under its sovereignty but left in the hands of the maharajas. On the threshold of independence they numbered 575. The colonists remained aloof from the Indians. They opposed local customs, imposed a legal system inspired by the British model and attempted to make English the national language, but they also opened schools, developed the railways and integrated India into the industrial revolution.

Path to Independence

The new Indian elite, educated in universities founded by the British, began to occupy administrative posts and claimed more and more social and cultural recognition. Its members bean to oppose the latent racism of the colonial authorities, censorship and conscription. The national Indian Congress movement, founded in 1885, soon made independence its battle cry. At the beginning of the 20th century, young Indian students like Mohandas Gandhi and Jawaharlal Nehru, came back from Britain imbued with notions of democracy and patriotism.

A dark cloud gathered over the horizon of the Empire. Gandhi organized his acts of civil disobedience and long marches: during the Salt March of 1930, he led an immense following to the sea shore to collect the salt which the British had claimed as their monopoly. The Mahatma's policy of passive resistance and Nehru's determination earned the two new Congress leaders several stays in prison, but also the support of the peasant masses. The world wars further tarnished the Europeans' image in the region, strengthening the nationalism of Indians who left to fight in Europe for the Union Jack.

Independence and Partition

As independence began to appear inevitable, so did a whole series of problems. The new India, for example, would have a Hindu majority, a situation that the Muslim minority considered intolerable. For many years, the leader

Gandhi on his way to the sea shore during the Salt March in 1930.

of the Muslims, Muhammad Ali Jinnah, had been calling for the division of the Empire into two distinct countries, India and Pakistan. Lord Mountbatten, dispatched to Delhi at the beginning of 1947 to settle the question, failed to make him change his mind. Already in 1946 an outbreak of civil war had resulted in 10,000 deaths of both Hindus and Muslims in Calcutta.

The proclamation of Indian Independence in August 1947 provoked an exodus of 12 million people. The new frontiers fuelled

The ancient lion capital of Ashoka's Pillar is the symbol of modern India.

istockphoto.com/Eromaze

Independent India

Ghandi, the figurehead of Independence, did not have everyone's support. Even today, Hindu nationalist groups reproach him for sacrificing India's politico-cultural tradition to British ideology, the institution of democracy having resulted in the partition of the country, the questioning of the social system and the reduction of the artisan classes to an impoverished proletariat. He was assassinated in 1948 by a Hindu extremist for having backed persecuted Muslims. Ali Jinnah, the Governor General of Pakistan, died the same year. His country was split into two regions 2,000 km (1,200 miles) apart, with a hostile India between them. It was not until 1971 that Eastern Pakistan proclaimed its independence and became Bangladesh. Because the region's industries remained on Indian soil, the new country was scarcely viable and the population miserably poor.

If it's true that India owes its independence to anglicized Indians, its economic expansion, agricultural progress and the stability of its institutions attest to the vitality of its democracy. The only threat the country has encountered since its creation is the personality cult surrounding the leaders of the Congress Party, in power almost without a break since 1947.

religious hatred: whole families of Muslims were murdered trying to reach Pakistan, while hundreds of thousands of Sikhs and Hindus suffered the same fate while trying to emigrate in the opposite direction.

The Rajput States accepted entry into the Indian Union, but Kashmir—with a large Muslim population but governed by Hindus—could not make a decision. Ever since, this territory has been the subject of clashes between the Indian and Pakistani armies.

Modern Times

The first of these leaders, Jawaharlal Nehru, served as prime minister from 1947 until his death in 1964. He was the great figurehead of the new India. Applying a socialist-orientedpolicy, he participated in the foundation of the Non-Aligned Movement. In 1966 he was succeeded by his daughter Indira Gandhi (no relation to Mahatma Gandhi). She drew closer to the Soviet Union, nationalized the banks, gave India atomic armament, promoted a productivist agriculture that enabled the country to achieve self-sufficiency in food and, in 1975, declared a state of emergency in order to counteract a decision of the justice to make her step down. Liberated from parliamentary restraints, she ruled by decree, imprisoned her opponents, muzzled the press and courted unpopularity with her programme of enforced sterilization. As a result she lost the 1977 elections, ousted by a coalition, but was recalled to power in 1980.

Dogged by intercommunal conflicts and rising corruption, Mrs Gandhi was soon confronted by demands for autonomy from the Sikhs, a minority religious group from the Punjab. To put down the insurrection, she ordered an attack on the Golden Temple, their high place of worship. She was assassinated in 1984 by her Sikh bodyguards.

Indira's son Rajiv Gandhi replaced her as the leader of the party and then as prime minister. As such, he reversed India's protectionist policies, liberalized the economy and drew closer to the US. This cost him his life. He sent the Indian Army to intervene in Sri Lanka against Tamil secessionists, who later assassinated him during an official visit. Meanwhile, his government had been accused of corruption and the Congress Party discredited.

In 1989, the party failed to win sufficient votes to form a government. The opposition took over in the 1990s. The Hindu nationalist Bharatiya Janata Party (BJP) came into power in 1998, returning at the head of a coalition the following year. In 2004 the BJP was defeated by the Congress Party under Rajiv's widow Sonia, but as the victim of a kabbala by the nationalist opposition denouncing her Italian origins, she was forced to refuse the position of prime minister, ceding it to Dr Manmohan Singh. The first Sikh to hold this office, he leads a coalition government, the United Progressive Alliance (UPA) and was re-elected in the general elections of May 2009. Sonia Gandhi remains leader of the Congress Party, carrying on the family tradition.

Ancient god, modern sticker: Shiva, the Destroyer, on a wall.

Dan Brady

RELIGIONS OF INDIA

The country has six principal beliefs. The population is composed of 80.5% Hindu, 13.4% Muslim, 2.3% Christian, 1.9% Sikh and less than 1% Buddhist and Jain. Religion is the key to understanding the people and their way of life.

Hinduism

For Hindus, the history of the world follows a cycle: the cosmos is born, dies and is reborn. There is no absolute beginning—thus no creator—and no end. Hinduism has no founder and no official clergy. The order of the universe serves as the absolute Truth.

Like every living thing, we all go through a series of rebirth and reincarnation. Our soul, however, is eternal. The final objective is *moksha*, the spiritual salvation that liberates the soul from this perpetual cycle in order to find *nirvana*, union with the Brahman. This state, or at least a better life, is reached thanks to our *karma* (the deeds and actions carried out to help the soul to progress); in effect, every good deed results in reincarnation at a higher level in the next cycle. The practice of yoga, which allows control of the body and elevation of the spirit, can also help us improve our karma.

The Hindu Pantheon

Hinduism is said to have 330 million deities. The figure serves to express the infinite nature of the Hindu pantheon: in fact 33 *koti* are listed, and this Sanskrit word has been interpreted as meaning 10 million. However, the number of gods is immaterial, since they are all emanations of the Brahman, the Absolute. They do not correspond in any way to the Western concept of a divinity.

The Hindu trinity *(trimurti)* comprises Brahma (the Creator), Vishnu (the Preserver) and Shiva (the Destroyer). Brahma, with four heads to represent his all-seeing presence, symbolizes the mind and intellect. He has only one significant temple in India, at Pushkar in Rajasthan. He is represented riding a *hamsa* (goose or swan). The other two are worshipped throughout the land. Shiva carries a trident and rides on the back of the bull Nandi. He wears a garland of skulls and has snakes writhing round his neck and arms. His emblem is the phallus, or *lingam*. Four-armed Vishnu flies around on the back of the eagle Garuda and is the only one of the three to be reincarnated. On his previous visits to earth he appeared in different forms, or avatars: for example as Krishna, Rama and even Buddha. His wife Lakshmi is the goddess of good fortune. Ganesh, the elephant-headed god of prosperity and wisdom, is the most popular, depicted with the rat that carries him around. Hanuman, the monkey god, an avatar of Shiva, is also very present. He is renowned for his strength, his loyalty to his spiritual master and his ability to repel demons and evil spirits.

Castes

Hindu society recognizes four castes: *Brahmans* (priests and the educated), *Kshatriyas* (rulers and warriors), *Vaisyas* (tradesmen and craftsmen) and *Sudras* (serfs). The consequence of this system is the uncomfortable situation of those who do not fit into any category, pariahs or "Untouchables" (whom Gandhi renamed *Harijan*, "children of god").

Originally, society was divided into guilds, but then 3,000 years ago the Brahmans introduced the notion of purity and awarded themselves the highest caste. Henceforth, activities considered to be "pure", for example contact with books, were accorded more importance than "impure" activities—such as shoemaking, which required the handling of dead animal skins.

Tika and Bindi. Most Hindus wear a *tika* (or *tilak*) between their eyes. This is the mark of their membership of the Hindu community. In the markets, you'll see heaps of red powder (*sindoor*), sacred ash (*vibhuti*) mixed with milk and ghee, sandalwood paste and cow dung which can all be used to make the product applied to the forehead by a priest as a sign of blessing as a dot or a line. Married women wear a *bindi* on their forehead as a protection against the evil eye, demons or bad luck. Stalls sell stick-on *bindi* like a fashion accessory.

istockphoto.com/Vardhan

Castes were officially abolished at Independence, but they continue to exist in the collective mind. In rural areas, marriage outside one's caste is still sometimes punishable by death. Women are still expected to bring a dowry, though the practice has been outlawed, and the majority of marriages are still arranged by the parents. In towns, however, the demands of the Untouchables for greater equality are gradually being heard. The former president of the Republic, K. R. Narayanan, was the first Untouchable to hold this office.

Islam

The second religion of the country, Islam was imposed by Muslim invaders in the 13th century. Today, with more than 162 million followers, India has the third-largest Muslim population in the world after Indonesia and Pakistan. Tensions between the Hindu and Muslim communities—which brought about the creation of Pakistan in 1947 and the massacres that ensued—continue to cause trouble on the subcontinent.

Jainism

One of the world's oldest religions, dating back at least 5,00 years, Jainism developed in India during the 6th century BC, as a reaction to Brahmanism—the precursor of Hinduism—and to

animal sacrifice. It owes a lot to the teachings of Mahavira (the great hero). He was the last of the *tirthankara*, a dynasty of 24 prophets, born in 599 BC. Like Buddha, he renounced his throne to lead a monastic life.

More than a religion, Jainism is an agnostic philosophy of life. It does not deny the existence of transcendent beings, but holds that direct intervention of gods or supernatural entities plays no part in the life of mankind. Man achieves perfection through his deeds. At death, he is reborn in another body, and the cycle continues until perfection is attained and he becomes at one with the Absolute.

The theory of *karma* and reincarnation comes from Jainism, as does belief in non-violence. The supreme commandment is to never harm any living creature—the natural consequence is vegetarianism. Pious Jains take the order to extremes: they may be seen wearing white linen masks to prevent any insect from entering their mouths, and picking their way carefully to avoid stepping on an ant.

There are two types of Jain: the *shvetambara* (clothed in white) and the *digambara* (clothed in "space"). In India, it is not unusual to meet Jain pilgrims walking naked by the edge of the road. They depend entirely on charity.

A guardian figure at a Buddhist temple in Sarnath.

Os Rúpias

Buddhism

Buddha, who took his inspiration from the practices and moral teachings of the Jains (reincarnation, for example), was born in India in the 5th century BC. He countered the many proscriptions of Brahmanism with simple virtues, such as goodness, charity and non-violence. He recommended the monastic life and renunciation of the world.

This humane doctrine, without mystery, spread rapidly and widely. A political blessing for those princes wishing to escape the power of the Brahman priests, it was largely supported by the noble and intellectual classes. Buddhism was to become a powerful cultural tool and the principal vehicle of Indian colonial expansion in Burma, Indochina, Indonesia, Tibet, Mongolia, China and even Japan. However, within India, it never reached the masses, who were too attached to their own rites and customs. Hinduism integrated the movement and broke its power by adopting Buddha as one of the avatars of Vishnu.

Sikhism

Sikh men ("disciples") are distinguished by their colourful turbans and uncut beards, often restrained by a hairnet. Sikhs make up only 1.9 per cent of the Indian population, but you frequently meet them in business circles or behind the wheel of a lorry or a taxi.

The Sikh religion, which has no clergy, was founded in the Punjab only at the beginning of the 16th century, by Guru Nanak. He adopted elements of Islam as well as Hinduism, claiming one unique God and rejecting the caste system, but conserving the theory of karma and reincarnation. Sikhs respect the rule of the five Ks: adepts all have long hair and beard *(kesh),* carry a comb *(kanga)* and a dagger *(kirpan)* and wear soldier's shorts *(kac-*

chera) and an iron bracelet (*kara*). They venerate the *Adi Granth*, a sacred book housed in the Golden Temple at Amritsar, the holy of holies of their religion. They are organized militarily and claim independence for the Punjab, their region of origin.

Parsiism

Inheritors of the Persian religion of Zoroastrianism, the Parsis came from Iran in the 8th century in order to escape persecution by the Muslims. They are today one of India's most prosperous and Europeanized groups, forming a diverse and strange congregation numbering fewer than 76,000 but controlling a large part of India's economy. Most of them live in or around Mumbai and in Gujarat. A community of sun worshippers, they keep a sacred and eternal flame hidden deep in their temples. They do not bury or cremate their dead but deliver them naked on the Towers of Silence for the vultures to devour.

Christianity and Judaism

Christianity came to India 500 years ago in the wake of the first ships and still clings on in the south, though it has never really gained a firm hold. The Jews have been in the south of India for more than 2,000 years.

Sacred Cows. Though the authorities of New Delhi are attempting desperately to rid the streets of cows, even implanting them with microchips and paying the citizens to round them up, you still see them here, there and everywhere. Every cow has an owner, but they are released every morning to forage from markets and dustbins in the streets.

The sanctity of the cow goes back to ancient times. During periods of famine, the cow was the only animal able to provide infants with a substitute for their mothers' milk. The Indians of the past, by making the cow the "mother of men" and endowing her with quasi-religious significance, ensured the survival of both their children and their "horned mothers".

According to Hindu mythology, the cow also assists the dead to cross the river leading to paradise. It would never occur to a Hindu to eat this symbol of universal motherhood. To kill one, furthermore, would inevitably lead to the worst of outlooks for the next life. This is why in some states refuges are provided for sick animals.

David Deivis

In the heart of Old Delhi, Chandni Chowk
(Silver Street) throbs with life, noise and
colour.

ON THE SCENE

From the capital to tiny villages deep within India, this guide reveals many faces of the North. Memories of the British Empire linger in New Delhi and Kolkata; Jaipur sings the exploits of the Rajput princes; Agra is resplendent with the works of Moghul emperors. Ancient Hindu culture discreetly hides its erotic temple carvings in the jungle of Madhya Pradesh. Meanwhile, the great gods of India watch the Ganges flow past the temples of Varanasi.

Delhi

Delhi is the centre of the world's largest democracy. In 1911, the British Indian Empire decided to transfer its capital from Calcutta (Kolkata) to this northern province and to build a gigantic, modern, imperial New Delhi next to the ancient Moghul city. This move was to symbolize the power of what the Prince of Wales could still call in 1931 "a solid Empire, sure and eternal".

Delhi's population has now passed the 17 million mark. The second-largest city of India after Mumbai, it comprises New Delhi, with all manner of traffic flowing beneath the flowering trees that border its avenues, and Old Delhi, noisy and bustling. Between the two is the Paharganj district.

Delhi is India's eternal capital, on a par with the holy city of Varanasi. It nurtured the dreams of all those who conquered the country, and has lived through seven dynasties. Seven cities preceded it, the oldest of which was built at least 2,600 years ago.

In the middle of the 20th century, before partition, Delhi had a strong Muslim population. Nowadays, Hindus are in the majority.

New Delhi

Well-ordered, airy and relatively quiet, New Delhi is the least Indian city in the country. You may come across a dromedary ambling along, and a couple of chattering monkeys might swing out of the trees as you pass by. But despite the colourful saris and the crowds of rickshaws, the capital cutivates its image of large modern metropolis. A dynamic city, no doubt, but you will soon start to notice its excesses and its drawbacks: traffic jams, dense crowds, pollution, dirty streets and endless road works.

Connaught Place

This immense square, named after the uncle of George V, is the lively centre of New Delhi. Comprising several concentric circles, it is home to many services, airline companies, travel agencies, banks and high-class restaurants frequented by businessmen and the wealthy bourgeoisie. The big hotels are a short walk away. Among them, the Imperial Hotel, framed by palm trees, has lost nothing of the charm which gave it its unique status during the days of the Raj.

Janpath (People's Way), one of the busiest avenues in the capital, starts at Connaught Place and leads south past the National Museum to the political centre.

Jantar Mantar

India's first observatory was built in 1724 on the orders of the Maharajah of Jaipur, Jai Singh II, an enthusiastic astronomer. He built four others, the most important of which is in his home city. The scientific measuring instruments, all pink, are scattered like huge geometrical sculptures around a garden designed for rest and recreation. Panels explain the function of each instrument: some are for foreseeing eclipses, others to measure time or to chart the stars and planets.

Humayun's Tomb

The tomb of the second ruler of the Moghul dynasty was a blueprint for the Taj Mahal. Whereas

Ampersandyslexia

Sugar and spice and all things nice. One of the most popular places in Delhi is **Nathu's pastry shop**, to the east of Connaught Place, in the middle of the Bengali Market. It is stocked with mountains of green or pale pink sweets, candied fruits, *gulab jamun* swimming in syrup, and pistachio, carrot or walnut creams heaped up on its counters. A thousand litres (2,100 pints) of milk and 500 kg (1,100 lb) of sugar go into their manufacture every day. The kitchens are worth a look.

the two monuments are of similar design and style, Humayun's Tomb, built in the 16th century, is less impressive and not as white as its famous marble counterpart. The development of architecture in India is associated with the reign of this emperor, and his tomb is one of the earliest examples of Moghul art in the country. Red sandstone cladding replaces the familiar Hindu sculpture and the inlay recalls that of Persian mausoleums.

Humayun's widow was responsible for the construction of this monument to the glory of her dead husband. As the Imperial couple had spent several years in exile in Kabul, the building was commissioned from a Persian architect, hence its style.

Its position in the middle of a garden was a novelty in India. The setting is magnificent. Flocks of parrots and swarms of squirrels have established residence in the branches of the ashoka trees, and this peaceful place is as charming as any walk in the countryside.

Purana Qila
North of Humayun's Tomb, the Purana Qila, or Old Fort, rises on the presumed site of the first Delhi. It was built during the first half of the 16th century. The **Sher Mandal**, a small octagonal tower of red sandstone, served as Humayun's library and observatory.

Indian children are always ready to smile for the camera.

Legend has it that it was while descending its staircase that the emperor slipped and lost his life. A mosque completes the architectural ensemble.

Crafts Museum
Just north of Purana Qila, this charming museum presents an overview of Indian crafts with furniture, sculpture, textiles and religious objects. Outside is an open-air museum where traditional houses from various regions have been gathered, and where demonstrations of crafts are given from October to June.

National Museum
One of India's biggest museums, it illustrates the riches of Indian art since prehistory until the Moghul period. You can admire vestiges of the Indus civilization, giant statues and bronze figures of Hindu deities, superb sections of Buddhist art and Indian minia-

tures, decorative arts, jewellery, manuscripts, paintings and all kinds of daily objects that would not be out of place in an ethnographic museum.

The Heart of Political India

The announcement of the decision to transfer the capital of British India to Delhi in 1911 took everyone by surprise. When the chief architect of the project, Sir Edward Lutyens, arrived from London in 1913, the King of England had already laid the foundation stone of the new city to the north of the old Moghul capital. Visiting the site on the back of an elephant, Lutyens, who was suffering from the heat, declared it poorly chosen. Returning under cover of darkness to dig up the royal stone, he decided to build the future Imperial capital to the south, near Raisina Hill.

A workforce of 30,000 men and women from all over northern India were hired to level the land, construct the roads and lay the drains. Apart from the official buildings, 4,000 residences were erected and 10,000 trees planted in 20 years. New Delhi was inaugurated on February 9, 1931, by the Viceroy, Lord Irwin, amidst parades of elephants and traditional Indian festivities. The party for 5,000 guests lasted for 15 days. Who could have imagined that only 16 years later the British would leave India forever?

Rashtrapati Bhavan

Dominating Rajpath, the Royal Road, the official residence of the President of the Republic is many times bigger than Buckingham Palace, with a façade 192 m (630 ft) long and a surface area of almost 19,000 sq m (204,000 sq

---

The Royal Road. Rajpath leads from India Gate to Rashtrapati Bhavan along a perfectly designed perspective. From the bedroom of his palace, the Viceroy of India could contemplate the triumphal arch behind which stood (at that time) a white marble statue of George V. Thus, the royal silhouette reminded the king's representative in India at his awakening every morning just who was the boss. The princes and members of the government whose homes also lined this road were equally brought to order by this sight. Conversely, when coming up Rajpath to visit the palace, they had their backs to the king. This gave them enough time to recover their self-confidence and thereby their ability to take decisions.

The statue of George V was removed in 1947, as were the other symbols of British domination. Since then, Rajpath is the scene of the parade marking Republic Day, every January 26.

ft). During the days of the British Empire, 2,000 servants worked here, 50 of whom were employed solely to chase unwelcome birds from the park. The interior can be visited on request, but only when the president is absent. The palace counts more than 300 rooms, including the immense teak dining room and the vast Darbar Hall, where the last British Viceroy, Lord Mountbatten, handed over power to the Prime Minister of India, Jawaharlal Nehru.

In the palace courtyard is the sandstone **Jaipur Column** 44 m (144 ft) high and surmounted by a lotus, presented to the British by the Maharajah of Jaipur as a token of the good relations between the princely states of Rajasthan and their conquerors.

The palace gardens are accessible in February and sometimes in March. Inspired by the Moghul gardens of Kashmir, they are filled with fountains and tended by 150 gardeners.

Ministries

Still on Raisina Hill, a group of buildings in perfect harmony with the architecture of Rashtrapati Bhavan surround the palace and confer upon it an impressive symmetry. Lutyens, who didn't much care for Hindu or Muslim architecture, chose a neoclassical Western style. He did, however, add a few Indian elements: the domes of the presidential palace are reminiscent of the Buddhist buildings which Lutyens admired. In fact, he himself described the ensemble as "an Englishman dressed for the climate". The stone, brought from the Agra region, and the surrounding earth are of the same ochre colour.

Today these buildings house the Ministry of Foreign Affairs and the Ministry of Finance. Columns in front of the façades represent the British Dominions: Australia, South Africa, Canada and New Zealand. The globes and ships surmounting the columns show the oceans traversed by the British and the countries they conquered.

Sansad Bhavan

The seat of the Indian Parliament, a circular building topped by a dome, lies to the northeast. It is home to the Rajya Sabha (Council of States) and the Lok Sabha (Chamber of the People). You can attend the debates by making a request for a permit at your embassy. To the left stands the Cathedral of the Redemption.

India Gate

At the far end of Rajpath, the India Gate is a triumphal arch 42 m (138 ft) high, built to honour the memory of the 90,000 Indian soldiers who fell during World War I, many in Europe.

Jawaharlal Nehru Memorial Museum

South of Raisina Hill, Teen Murti House, the mansion where Nehru lived, has been converted into a museum. The garden is famous for its roses — Nehru always wore a rose in his buttonhole. Nothing has been altered since the death of the great man in 1964.

Indira Gandhi Memorial Museum

Leaving Teen Murti House by Murti Marg you reach Safdarjung Road. Number 1 is Mrs Gandhi's bungalow, but it has nothing of the splendour you might expect of a prime minister's residence. Nehru's daughter was assassinated by her bodyguards in the garden in October 1984.

Tomb of Safdarjung

Southwest of New Delhi, this is the last mausoleum to have been built during the Moghul era (1754). It is surrounded by beautiful gardens of Persian inspiration and is topped by a huge onion dome. The nearby **Lodhi Gardens** are a haven for anyone looking for shade, roses and greenery in the middle of the city. Other tombs in the area predate those of the Moghuls.

Lotus Temple

The Bahai movement opened this monumental temple in the southeast of New Delhi in 1996. Sym-

Gandhi's assassination. The Mahatma often stayed with the Birlas family, in Tees January Road (their house is now a museum, the **Hall of the Nation**). Gandhi, known as "Bapu", or father by the people, was not popular with all Hindus. Some reproached him for defending the Untouchables, others for having accepted partition and for supporting the Muslims. Those Muslims not yet expatriated to Pakistan had been persecuted throughout the country since the declaration of Independence. On their behalf Gandhi undertook his last campaign at the end of 1947. Following a fast designed to stir up public opinion, he was murdered by a Hindu fanatic when he went to pray in the Birlas's garden.

Diganta Talukdar

bolizing a communion of all religions, it is built in the shape of a lotus flower and is surrounded by an expansive park.

Qutb Minar

Constructed around 1200 by the first Sultan of Delhi, the Qutb (or Qutab) Minar south of New Delhi has a 5-storey minaret, 72 m (236 ft) high. It is a UNESCO World Heritage site, but has been closed to the public since a stampede on the stairs in 1981 caused the death of 40 people.

In the courtyard of the nearby mosque, the 7-m (22-ft) **Iron Pillar** dates from the 4th century. Made from a metal of exceptional purity, it has not rusted after centuries of monsoon rains. The pillar is said to bring good luck to anyone who can stand with his back to it and encircle it with their arms.

Old Delhi

The seventh and penultimate Delhi is a Moghul city. Its monuments are essentially the work of one man, Shah Jahan, who transferred his capital here from Agra in 1648. Often compared to Louis XIV for his extravagance and taste for power, the "King of the World" had just completed the famous Taj Mahal. His legacies to Delhi are the Friday Mosque and Lal Qila, the Red Fort. The fort is now a lifeless pile. But you'll find something of the sparkle of the old days in the tangle of lanes of the old town, filled with the noise of sputtering engines. There are still many Muslims living here,

Youngrobv

The Qutb Minar, built to the orders of India's first Muslim ruler.

especially around the mosque. It is magical, disconcerting — in short, typically Indian.

Lal Qila

It took nine years for Shah Jahan to build his fort. The Moghul Empire was at the summit of its power and the architecture of this symmetrical, rectangular building reflects the image of a solidly established monarchy. The white marble walls were inlaid with precious stones, the ceilings gleamed with silver and gold, and carpets covered the courtyards.

A symphony of arches in the Red Fort's Diwan-i-Am.

Alnis

Rose-scented water supplied the royal baths to the left of the palace. Nearby, "monsoon fountains" sprinkled "rain" in the dry season, and a ventilation system cooled the air.

What is left standing today can give only a vague idea of the original, as the British demolished most of the apartments and replaced them with barracks. When they took Delhi in 1803, they found the Moghul emperor shut away in this last bastion of an empire that had endured for nearly three centuries. Fifty-four years later, the Red Fort was to become the setting for scenes from the Indian Mutiny. The massive gates at the western entrance are still pockmarked with the bullet holes.

You enter by the pink sandstone **Lahore Gate**, which opens directly into a bazaar which was originally the shopping area for the ladies of the court.

The emperor would hear complaints from his subjects in the **Diwan-i-Am**, the Hall of Public Audience, where he sat cross-legged on a throne beneath a canopy. At the back of the hall are panels inlaid with birds and flowers.

Private meetings were held by appointment in the **Diwan-i-Khas**. Here the emperor sat on a splendid solid gold Peacock Throne. Only the marble pedestal remains today; the throne was taken to Iran by the Persian troops of Nadir Shah in 1739 and broken up. The silver ceiling was also removed, but you can still see on the walls the famous couplet: "If there is a paradise on earth, it is this, it is this, it is this!"

The main harem, **Rang Mahal** (Palace of Colour) has ceiling and walls ornamented with mirror mosaics which twinkle like stars if you strike a match.

Jama Masjid

The Friday Mosque, the biggest in India, was the last indulgence of Shah Jahan. The courtyard can hold 25,000 people, and the striped minarets of white marble and red sandstone measure 40 m (over 130 ft). Stalls and workshops look lost at the foot of the monumental staircases, and the whole area seems overwhelmed by the white marble domes striped with black. Seething with people and animals, the surrounding lanes have lost nothing of their timeless charm, especially seen by lamplight.

Chandni Chowk

The main thoroughfare and the heart of Old Delhi was once a processional avenue. Starting just opposite the Red Fort, Chandni Chowk (Silver Street) stretches from the small Jain temple of **Lal Mandir** (1656) in the east to **Fatehpuri Mosque**, built in 1650 by one of Shah Jahan's wives, at its western end. Half-way between the two is **Sunehri Masjid**, the Golden Mosque. In 1739 Nadir Shah climbed onto the roof to watch his troops massacre the district's inhabitants.

There is nothing much left of the merchants' luxurious homes and the expensive shops which gave Chandni Chowk its reputation as the greatest shopping centre in the east. Nevertheless, the famous street and the maze of lanes running from it remain unrivalled for strolling at the end of the day among the thousands of shops, stalls and bazaars of all descriptions selling clothes, jewellery and traditional sweetmeats.

Over the Yamuna River

The **Swaminarayan Akshardam Temple** was consecrated in 2005. Linked to a Hindu movement implanted in the Gujarat area, it pays homage to the guru Swaminarayan (1781–1830), deified in the form of a gilded sculpture, or *murti*, 3 m (10 ft) tall, beneath a ceiling studded with precious stones. The huge building of pink sandstone and white marble is surrounded by an impressive elephant terrace.

Metromania. The first Delhi metro opened for business on Christmas Day, 2002. There were only six stops at that time, on the route from Shahadra to Tis Hazari in the north of the city, near the Kashmere Gate. But more than 150,000 people turned up to check out the gleaming new trains, making it more like a festival than a metro line. The first phase of the network, with three lines, was completed at the end of 2005, with several more lines to be built by 2020. Delhiites are immensely proud of this feat of engineering, which has brought a dash of modernity to their city.

The streets of Jaisalmer's lower town are lined with *haveli* carved from golden sandstone.

Northern Rajasthan and Jodhpur

Stretching from the Shekawati region, 200 km (125 miles) southwest of Delhi, to the splendid isolation of Jaisalmer near the western border with Pakistan, Northern Rajasthan is a land of infinite semi-desert scenery and dazzling Rajput towns. Indeed, it seems at times as if the Rajasthani people have sought to temper the bleakness of the desert landscape with an extravagant show of bright colours, be it in their brilliantly dyed clothes, the famous painted palaces of Shekawati, or whole towns known by their prevalent colour, such as the blue of Jodhpur and golden Jaisalmer.

This is the heartland of historic Rajputana, that dangerous frontier territory ruled by the warlike Rajputs since the 7th century. There were several different ruling clans, each of whom jealously guarded their own territory, which explains why every hill seems to have a fortress perched on it and each town you visit is packed with more than its fair share of luxurious palaces. There are plenty of opportunities to trek out into the empty expanse of the desert on camelback.

Shekawati

This sandy, semi-arid region in the north of Rajasthan contains more than a few surprises. At first sight it appears to be utterly desolate, its dry soil resistant to the efforts of human cultivation. And yet it is dotted with small towns that contain perhaps the most concentrated collection of murals in India.

It was only in the 15th century that the area began to achieve prominence, thanks largely to its strategic position on the increasingly important trade route between Delhi and the seaports of Gujarat. At the time it was ruled by the Rajah of Amber. However, an independent kingdom soon emerged under Rao Shekha, after whom the region is named. By the 18th century, the Shekawati was at its zenith, with its merchants enjoying considerable riches from the flourishing caravan routes. The arrival of the British put an end to the good times. The development of Bombay and Calcutta as major trading ports, and the use of the railways to transport goods, meant that Shekawati was effectively bypassed. True to their resilient Rajput roots, the Shekawati merchants simply moved to where the business was, setting up home in the new trading centres and becoming some of India's most successful moneymakers.

A considerable part of their wealth was channelled back to their home towns and spent on lavish palaces, known as *haveli*.

Street graphics: shop sign for lamps becomes modern art.

Meena Kadri

No expense was spared, and they were covered with sumptuous paintings. These haven't always fared well over the years, and the effects of the harsh climate have been compounded in some cases by wilful neglect. But there are enough superb sights left to make a tour of the region an exciting voyage of discovery.

Mandawa

In the centre of the Shekawati, Mandawa is a popular little market town with a cluster of notable *haveli*.

At the western end of the town, the **Goenka Double Haveli** has a fine group of elephants and horses painted over the façade. The Goenkas were one of the region's best-known merchant families. Another of their residences, the **Hanuman Prasad Goenka Haveli** can be seen nearby. It's also worth seeking out the murals and mosaics of the **Saraf Haveli**, a short walk south of here.

At the heart of Mandawa is an 18th-century Rajput fort. Now a hotel, you can cool off here with a drink and enjoy excellent views of the town from the terrace.

Bikaner

Located 200 km (124 miles) west of Mandawa, Bikaner has developed around a spectacular fort and a walled old town. Established as the capital of a separate kingdom in 1488 by Rao Bika, son of the ruler of Jodhpur, the city flourished as a result of its position at the edge of the great Thar Desert, as traders from the Middle East bound for Delhi would stop here in need of sustenance after the difficult journey. Like the towns of the Shekawati, it too suffered from the rise of Bombay and Calcutta under the British Raj. A new lease of life was given during the rule of Maharaja Ganga Singh (1880–1943), who created the renowned Bikaner Camel Corps and built the Ganga Canal in the 1920s, a vitally important irrigation channel for this arid region.

In the maze of streets in the old town, you will come across some splendid *haveli* (mansions) with finely sculpted façades, such as **Bhanwar Niwas**, converted into a hotel. A little further on the Hindu **Laksminath temple**, five centuries old, stands next to the Jain **Bhandasar temple** (1468), with a splendid group of polychrome sculptures.

Junagarh Fort

Unlike most Rajasthani forts, the one in Bikaner does not stand on a hilltop, but this doesn't make it any less imposing. With its 37 bastions and towering ramparts 12 m (39 ft) high, the fort dominates the centre of town. Built by Raja Rai Singh in the late 16th century, it has never been conquered.

The palace-fort complex is entered via three huge gates. By the second one, pause to see the hand prints sculpted in relief of the rajahs' wives who practised sati, or self-immolation after the death of their husbands. The **Karan Mahal** (Hall of Public Audience) dates from 1680 and has lovely frescoes and a gilt ceiling. Pass from here to the splendid **Anup Mahal**, with the throne where the maharajas were crowned. The room is a riot of gilt, mirrorwork mosaics and painted tiles. Beyond the throne room, you enter the **Badal Mahal** chamber, painted blue with white clouds striped

Avid Hills

Rats rule. The temple of Karni Mata lies near **Deshnoke,** 30 km (19 miles) south of Bikaner. Karni Mata was a 15th-century saint and mystic from the Charans caste, which was made up of storytelling bards. When her request to Yama, the god of death, to revive a dead Charans child was rejected, she decreed that all Charans from that time onwards would be reincarnated in her temple as rats. In this way they would avoid Yama claiming their human souls. As a result, in this temple the rodent is king. Cosseted by priests and pilgrims alike, who pamper them with milk and sweets, the rats are, you'll be pleased to discover, as unthreatening a bunch as you could hope to meet. And if you happen to see a white one, consider yourself especially lucky, as they are supposed to be auspicious.

with lightning — an exotic theme for these arid parts of the world. Go upstairs for a panorama of the ramparts and gardens. You will come to the superb bedroom of the maharajah Gaj Singh Manda containing a ritual mechanical swing used for the anniversary of the god Krishna. Further on, past the armoury, the conference room, **Ganga Niwas**, houses a sandalwood canopied throne. The visit ends with the **museum**, containing mementoes of Ganga Singh (desk, uniforms, paintings) and a World War I bi-plane, a gift of the British government.

Within the walls of the fort, the **Prachina Cultural Centre and Museum** displays objects illustrating the daily life of the maharajas: costumes, portraits, furniture, ox-carts and so on.

Lalgarh Palace

The red sandstone palace, 2 km (just over a mile) northeast of the fort, was built in 1900 for Ganga Singh. One of its wings is still a royal residence, while the others house two hotels. It also contains the **Sri Sadul Museum**. Apart from a royal carriage it has an eclectic range of artefacts relating to the lives of the maharajas, with hundreds of photos of ceremonies and tiger-hunting and the 100 kg brass *tokna*, a pot that was carried around the state by camel and used for collecting taxes.

Ganga Golden Jubilee Museum

East of the fort, this museum has a small collection of paintings, musical instruments, models and sculptures, including a superb 11th-century marble figure of Sarasvati.

Camel Breeding Farm

A visit to the National Research Centre on Camels, 10 km (6 miles) south of town, is a unique experience. Every day at around 4 p.m. a caravan of hundreds of animals return to their stables: a majestic spectacle.

Jaisalmer

Seemingly marooned in the empty expanse of the Thar desert 330 km (205 miles) southwest of Bikaner, the Golden City of Jaisalmer rises out of the desert like a mirage. The honey-coloured ramparts of its mighty fortress loom over the landscape, while the maze of ancient streets have lost none of their power to draw the visitor into another world.

The city and fortress were founded in 1156 by Rao Jaisal of the Rajput Bhatti clan, when he decided to move his capital from Lodrava, 15 km (9 miles) away, to this more strategic hilltop location. The Bhattis added to their wealth by the odd spot of caravan-raiding, but when at the beginning of the 14th century they unwisely looted one belonging to the Sultan of Delhi, his response was to lay waste to the town. In the 16th century, the Bhattis settled down under the Moghuls to the more peaceful business of turning their city into a major trading centre. Left a backwater by the rise of Bombay under the British, the city seemed ready to fade into oblivion, until it was rediscovered by tourists in the 1960s, and then given another financial boost by the increased presence of the Indian military in the region following the war with nearby Pakistan in 1971.

Fort

Perched dramatically on Trikurta Hill, which culminates at 100 m (328 ft), the fort is enclosed by an outer wall and two rings of battlements, which are in turn protected by 99 bastions. The great boulders you can see were placed here ready to be tipped onto unwary besiegers. The walls and terraces offer magnificent views of the lower town and the surrounding desert.

The fort is in fact a town within a town. You reach it via an S-shaped ramp in the northeast, interrupted by four monumental gateways. It opens onto a square overlooked by the maharajah's palace, **Raj Mahal**. Belying its beautifully decorated façade, built in the 16th century, the interior is considerably more under-

Srinavan Puppala

Contestant for the best-dressed camel competition, Jaisalmer.

stated in style. A veritable labyrinth of halls and smaller rooms clustered over seven floors, it has kept some handsome carved doors and is the setting for several historic dioramas. Don't miss the splendid silver lion's throne, decorated with wild beasts and peacocks, used during coronations.

Beyond the palace, a maze of narrow streets and alleyways contain shops, houses and temples bathed in silence: motor vehicles are banned. A short stroll southwest of the palace takes you to an extraordinary group of seven **Jain** temples, built by rich merchants of the community between the end of the 15th and beginning of the 16th centuries. They are dedicated to different *tirthankara* (prophets) and so closely welded together they seem as one. The *apsaras*, deities, dragons and floral motifs covering every inch of the carved stone are exquisite in their finesse.

Lower Town

To the north, the lower town contains a number of magnificent *haveli*, which date from the 18th and 19th centuries and are an expression of the private wealth accrued by the city's merchants. The most impressive is the Patwon ki Haveli, comprising five contiguous mansions built for the five sons of a Jain merchant. Its spectacularly ornate façade took more than 50 years to complete. One of the five houses hosts a private museum with restored interiors; it displays fascinating historic collections. Another, managed by the local government, is a beautiful but empty shell. Nearby, Nathmal ki Haveli, another masterpiece of intricate carving, is guarded by two sandstone elephants that once signalled the homes of the prime ministers. You might also like to visit Salim Singh ki Haveli, poorly maintained but with a marvellous upper loggia with peacock carvings.

Southeast of the ramparts, Tilon ki Pol, a handsome carved sandstone doorway, built around 1900 by a famous prostitute, opens onto the Garisar pool. Created in the 14th century to provide water for the city, it has an elegant group of floating pavilions.

Camel Safaris

Jaisalmer is well-known as a centre for camel safaris. Popular trips go out to the dunes of Sam, 40 km (25 miles) to the west and those of Khuri 45 km (28 miles) south. Shorter excursions take you to the maharajahs' cenotaphs at Bada Bagh, the maharajah's garden and Jain temple of Amar Sagar, both places 6 km (4 miles) from Jaisalmer, or further east, the old capital of Lodruva, 15 km (9 miles) away. It was anterior to Jaisalmer. Its splendid Jain shrine, rebuilt in the 16th century, is said to have a cobra living beneath the foundations, feeding on the daily offerings of milk.

Osiyan

It's hard to believe now, but between the 8th and 12th centuries this dusty little desert town around 240 km (150 miles) due east of Jaisalmer was a thriving commercial hub. It was also a centre for the Jain and Hindu religions. Though its heyday is long gone, people still come today to see its historic temples.

Sachiya Mata Temple

The original 8th-century Hindu temple was destroyed by Mongol invaders but was rebuilt, probably in the 12th century. Sachiya Mata was also known as Indrani, the consort of the rain and war god Indra; she is also assimilated with the mother goddess, and just beyond the entrance are several sandstone sculptures representing her. On a hill, the main shrine of the temple is topped by a dome decorated with beautifully carved *apsaras*, or celestial maidens. Just outside, the two small shrines covered with erotic sculptures are dedicated to Ganesh and Shiva.

Mahavira Temple

A short walk away, this superb temple was built on a terrace by the Jains in the 8th century. The entrance is carved with two gazelles. As with the Hindu temple, the pillars and dome of the main chamber, or *gudha-mandapa*, are intricately sculpted. In the inner sanctum you'll see an ancient statue of Mahavira, the last of the 24 Jain prophets, coated in gold leaf and said to have been made from a mixture of sand and milk. The side shrines, also prettily carved, are dedicated to other prophets.

Jodhpur

The Blue City—so-called because of the number of houses

hemis.fr/Morandi

Under the gaze of Shiva, a multi-coloured street in Jodhpur, the Blue City.

painted in that colour—is the second-largest in Rajasthan, 63 km (39 miles) south of Osiyan. It's a lively place, teeming with traders and tourists alike. Jodhpur was founded in 1459 by the Rajput king Rao Jodha, who made it the capital of the state of Marwar. Placed under Moghul protection, the city maintained peaceful links with the emperors and offered them several great generals. In 1679, Aurangzeb put an end to its autonomy, retrieved after his death in 1707.

A true blue town. No one seems to know why so many houses in Jodhpur are painted blue. Possibly it has something to do with the Hindu association of this colour with the Divine. The priestly Brahmins used it to mark out their homes from those belonging to the lower castes, and perhaps the good people of Jodhpur simply decided that, Brahmin or not, they were entitled to their own piece of heaven. Others have suggested it's for more pragmatic reasons, however—the colour blue is commonly thought to repel heat and mosquitoes.

Renata Holzbachová

Jodhpur's **old town** is full of bustling bazaars, especially renowned for silverware, textiles and spices. At their centre is a distinctive clock tower, dating from the British era.

Mehrangarh Fort

The highpoint of Jodhpur, inevitably, is the "Majestic Fort", built on a ridge 125 m (410 ft) high. Its towering walls and magnificent courtyards and palaces exemplify the power and grandeur of the Rajput princes. The first of seven gates is Jai Pol, which commemorates the defeat of the Maharaja of Jaipur's army in 1806. Beyond this, next to the Loha Pol gate, are handprints of the widows of Maharaja Man Singh, who carried out *sati* by throwing themselves upon their husband's funeral pyre, in 1843.

The palaces of the fort now make up the **Mehrangarh Museum**. In the first room of the Moti Mahal (Palace of Pearls) you can admire a fine collection of elephant howdahs, some in elaborate repoussée silver. Beyond this are rooms containing a group of palanquins, princely costumes, and a delightful collection of Rajasthani miniature paintings. Upstairs, the Phool Mahal (Palace of Flowers) is a stunning 18th-century reception hall covered in frescoes, stained glass and vast amounts of gold leaf. The Takhat Vilas housed the apartments of Maharaja Takhat Singh and dates from the mid-19th century. Note the murals and lovely sandalwood inlay on the ceiling.

The ladies' quarters were in the Jankhi Mahal (Palace of

Glances), whose latticework windows permitted them to see but not be seen. The room houses an exhibition of cradles in which the infant maharajas of Jodhpur once slumbered.

Ramparts

Before you leave the fort, head for the southern end of the ramparts, where the view over the Blue City is magical, especially in the late-afternoon sunshine.

As you descend, look out to the northeastern side of the fort for the white marble **Jaswant Thada**, a cenotaph built in 1899 on the cremation site of Maharaja Jaswant Singh II.

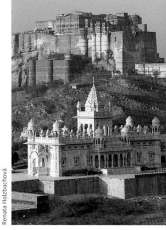

Renata Holzbachová

Mehrangarh Fort is as majestic as its name suggests.

Once more unto the breeches...

The leggings of choice for discerning horse-riders the world over, jodhpurs were named after the distinctive trousers worn by the polo-playing Pratap Singh, Maharaja of Jodhpur. Tight at the ankle and baggy at the thighs, they were in fact the traditional riding gear used by the Marwari cavalry. British army officers, who first encountered polo in India and played it alongside the maharaja, immediately saw the practicality of wearing them in the saddle. Before long, the British had taken the maharaja's game, name and breeches for themselves.

Umaid Bhawan Palace

Further out, the enormous pink sandstone palace was built on Chittar Hill, the highest point in Jodhpur, between 1927 and 1944 for the Maharaja Umaid Singh. With 347 rooms, it is one of the world's largest private residences: one section is reserved for the current maharaja, while the rest is divided between a luxury hotel and a small museum open to the public, with a collection of clocks, porcelain, weaponry and mementoes from the 19th-century heyday of the maharajas.

Rendered in silk, all the splendour of the maharana and his suite.

Udaipur and Southern Rajasthan

Unlike the mainly arid terrain in the north of the state, southern Rajasthan has a far greater variety of landscape, ranging from fertile valleys and huge artificial lakes to the lush jungle around Ranthambore, near its eastern border with Madhya Pradesh. There's also a great diversity in the places to visit. You can enjoy the sights and sounds of the famous Pushkar camel fair, go tiger-watching in the Ranthambore National Park, or escape the heat of the plains in the old Raj hill station on Mount Abu. But one sight no one should miss is Udaipur, a town of legendary beauty and romance.

Udaipur

Surrounded by hills and forests, and with its enchanting yellow-walled palaces perched picturesquely on Lake Pichola, Udaipur is a feast for the eye. The town was established as the capital of the princely state of Udaipur in 1568, when the Maharana Udai Singh was forced out of his Chittorgarh stronghold by the armies of the Moghul Emperor Akbar. The Aravalli Hills to the north provided natural defences against subsequent Moghul attacks, and the town was able to maintain its independence. Like many other Rajput princes, the maharanas of Udaipur enjoyed stability during the 19th century under British protection. Following Indian independence, Udaipur joined the new state of Rajasthan.

City Palace

The old town is dominated by the spectacular City Palace, which runs parallel to the edge of the lake. Begun under Udai Singh more than 400 years ago, the palace was added to and altered right up to the 20th century. Despite this, the variations in architectural style achieve a triumphantly harmonious blend of turrets, towers and balconies. It now houses the excellent **City Palace Museum**. You can enter through either the Badi Pol, a gate dating from 1616, or the Tripolia Gate, built in 1725. Here you'll find the eight marble arches where the maharanas used to be weighed, and their equivalent weight in silver or gold given out to their subjects.

The museum features a well-stocked armoury and a fine collection of miniature paintings. Many of the rooms upstairs are works of art in themselves. The Chini Mahal is decorated with Delft porcelain tiles, while the Moti Mahal is studded with semi-precious stones and mirrorwork, and the Manak Mahal displays glass and porcelain figurines. Note the gold statue representing Surya, the sun god, in the Surya Chaupar: the ruling Sisodia dynasty trace their lineage back

Henrik Bennetsen

Daniel Wabyick

to this deity (indeed, the name Udai means "sunrise").

In the **Queen's Palace**, next door, you'll find paintings and palanquins, a 1920s Rolls-Royce, and great views of the lake.

Crystal Gallery

Nearby, against the lake shore, another palace in this huge complex — the Fateh Prakash Palace, now a hotel — is linked to the celebrated Crystal Gallery. This extraordinary collection includes not only chandeliers and lamps, but also tables and beds made out of crystal. They were all ordered in 1877 from Osler's of Birmingham by the Maharana Sajjan Singh, who sadly died before they arrived. Visit the opulent durbar hall (reception room), with its huge bell-shape chandeliers and portraits of past maharanas.

Old Town

The rest of the old town is extremely pleasant to stroll around. Just to the north of the City Palace, the **Jagdish Temple** was built in 1651. There are some superb carvings on the outer walls, and

Renata Holzbachová

Floating opposite the City Palace, Udaipur's famous Lake Palace covers a whole island. | Crystal peacock in the City Palace Museum. | Women, children and images of Isar (Shiva) and Gauri (Parvati) at the Gangaur festival.

inside the main shrine is a black statue of Vishnu in his incarnation as Jaganath, Lord of the World.

Go down to the shore and **Gangaur Ghat**, where you'll see pretty havelis and small shops. In the late afternoon, you can head to **Sunset Point**, located in Manakya Lal Verma park south of the City Palace, for scenic lake views.

Lake Pichola

The lake provides a wonderful backdrop to Udaipur's palaces. It was originally created from a river that was dammed at this point. Enlarged by Udai Singh, it now covers 12 sq km (almost 5 sq miles). There are two islands, both of which can be reached by boat from the City Palace jetty. **Jag Niwas** is entirely taken up by the sumptuous **Lake Palace**, which now houses one of the world's most famous luxury hotels. It was built from white marble in 1746 and used as the summer palace of the maharanas.

The other island, **Jag Mandir**, is a little to the south. The Islamic-style sandstone and marble palace here dates from the early 17th century, and its appearance might well have influenced the Moghul Emperor Shah Jahan, future builder of the Taj Mahal, who used it as a refuge in 1623 after an unsuccessful rebellion against his father, Jahangir. Eight imposing white marble elephants guard the boat ramp and entrance to the palace, which has lovely gardens and a black-and-white tiled courtyard. The complex includes a mosque and a restaurant—and is a popular place for weddings.

Mount Abu

Located on a high plateau 185 km (115 miles) west of Udaipur in the Aravalli Range, the small town of Mount Abu was developed as a hill station by the British, who would come here to cool off during the furnace-like heat of Rajasthan's summer months. It retains the air of a holiday retreat to this day, and at times such as school vacations it becomes especially noisy and crowded. But this is more than offset by the fine panoramas, pleasure-boat rides on Nakki Lake and the temples at Dilwara, among the most elaborately decorated in northern India.

Dilwara

The magnificent Jain temples of Dilwara, 5 km (3 miles) from the town, pre-date Mount Abu's role as a tourist resort by several centuries. They were built from white marble, and then sculpted by craftsmen at the peak of their art. Two of them are particularly outstanding.

Vimal Vasahi Temple dates from the first half of the 11th century. A fairly sober façade gives way

Black-faced langur meditates in Kumbalgarh Wildlife Sanctuary.

Zen Skillicorn

to an extraordinary interior of exquisitely carved columns, 57 arched cells, each with a statue of a Jain *tirthankara* (one of the founders of the religion), and the entrance of the elephant pavilion, with a procession of sculpted elephants.

The **Tejpal Temple** was built in the 13th century and is, if anything, even more richly decorated. The artistry of the marble carvings on the pillars and in the dome of the *ranga mandapa* (dance pavilion) is little short of miraculous.

To end the day, you can enjoy the golden hour as the sun goes down from **Sunset and Honeymoon Point** in the west of town.

Kumbhalgarh

The mighty fort of Kumbhalgarh rises over the thickly forested foothills of the Aravalli Range, 85 km (53 miles) north of Udaipur. Built by the Rana Kumbha in the early 15th century, it was one of the most important fortresses of the ancient Mewar kingdom, prior to Maharana Udai Singh's retreat southwards in the face of Moghul expansion. With its commanding hilltop position and thick walls, it was nigh on impregnable, falling only once to the Moghuls in the 1570s after the enemy forces poisoned the water supply. Its ramparts, 36 km (22 miles) in perimeter, are studded with round bastions and pierced by seven gates. After the palaces of Udaipur were built, the maharanas turned their backs on this remote spot until the 19th century, when Maharana Fateh Singh had the fort renovated.

Inside the ramparts, only a few of the 365 temples remain intact. This makes it a hauntingly quiet place, with few of the usual commercial trappings of Rajasthan's popular fortress towns; a good deal of the mysterious atmosphere of a lost city floats about it. Just inside the Hanuman Gate, the restored 15th-century three-storey **Vedi Temple** was used for sacrifices. Kumbha worshipped daily in **Nilkanth Mahadev**, which is much older than all the other temples and has slender fluted pillars. Fateh Singh pulled down Rana Kumbha's palace and replaced it with another fort, **Kartargarh**, inside which you can see some remains of the original temples and shrines. The complex is crowned by **Badal Mahal**, the Cloud Palace of the Ranas, also built by Fateh Singh. From here you can look out over the whole fort, its ramparts spreading far into the surrounding jungle.

Wildlife Sanctuary

The forest below the fort has become a sanctuary where wolves, leopards and panthers prowl and chowsinghas, a four-horned antelope, try their best to avoid them.

Chittorgarh

The ancient capital of the Mewar kingdom lies about 100 km (60 miles) northeast of Udaipur. It was founded in the 8th century by the Sesodia Rajputs and survived several attacks until the fateful onslaught of Akbar's troops in 1568. The defenders went out to certain death against the Moghul armies while the women and children chose *jauhar*—mass immolation—rather than surrender. The Maharana Udai Singh managed

to slip away and build a new capital at Udaipur. Despite being reclaimed in the following century, Chittorgarh was never resettled. Today, however, the town is as bustling as any in Rajasthan.

Fort

Between the second and third of the seven defensive gates, two *chhatris* (cenotaphs) commemorate the teenage heroes Jaimal and Kalla, who died in the struggle against Akbar in 1568. Inside the fort are the ruins of several historic palaces and temples. The 15th-century **Rana Kumbha Palace** was severely damaged during Akbar's attack. Part of the original façade has survived, along with remains of the Diwan-i-Am and elephant stables. Nearby are two temples contemporary with the palace, and another of Fateh Singh's more recent additions, the **Fateh Prakash Palace**, which houses a small museum.

The most striking monument is the **Tower of Victory**, 37 m (121 ft) high, erected in the 1460s by Kumbha to celebrate his military victory over the Sultan of Malwa in southeastern Rajasthan. Close by, the **Maha Sati** was where the Maharanas were cremated. This is also where many of the women of Chittorgarh carried out *jauhar* in 1568.

The smaller, older **Tower of Fame** was put up in the 12th century by

Pushkar has 52 ghats, each with its own
miraculous powers of healing.

Huber/Sitla

a Jain merchant to honour Adi-natha, the first Jain *tirthankara*. Not far from here, **Padmini's Palace** was home to a princess of the early 14th-century. You can still see the gardens and *zenana* (women's quarters) of the palace.

Ajmer

At the very edge of the Aravalli Range 190 km (118 miles) north of Chittorgarh, Ajmer is one of the main sites of Muslim pilgrim-age in India. It owes this status to the Afghan leader Muhammad of Ghor, who took over the town in the 12th century and made it an important centre of Islam.

Dargah Khwaja Moinuddin Chisti

In 1192, the Sufi divine Khwaja Moinuddin Chisti arrived in Aj-mer charged with a mission to convert the inhabitants to Islam. He carried out this task so well that he was soon revered as a saint. His *dargah* (tomb) soon became one of the main Islamic sites in India, especially vener-ated by the Moghul emperors, who were mostly responsible for its construction. The shrine is accessible to non-Muslims re-specting Islamic dress rules. It in-cludes shelters for pilgrims, small shops and kitchens where two huge cauldrons simmer to pro-vide food for the crowds that come on special days. There are also two mosques, one built by

Akbar (1570), the other by Shah Jahan—the **Jami Masjid** (1640)—framing the small tomb of the saint under its marble dome. Wor-shippers avidly throw heaps of rose petals over the sepulchre.

On a hill, about 400 m (440 yd) away, stand the ruins of **Adhai din ka Jhonpra**, the "two-and-a-half-day" mosque. Dating from the 13th century, they have preserved a prayer room with tall heavily decorated columns taken from Jain or Hindu temples. All the carved figures were quite literally defaced when the mosque was built—in two and a half days.

Akbar's Fort

Built around 1560 by emperor Akbar, the fort was the scene of the first meeting between a Mo-ghul ruler, Jahangir, and a British ambassador. It houses a modest museum.

Mayo College

In 1874, the British, in their desire to form the Indian élite, inaugurated this university in neo-Moghul style, soon known as the "Eton of India". Originally only the sons of maharajas were admitted. Their fathers built the luxurious residences still to be seen amdst the golf courses, cricket grounds and polo fields. Nowadays the students also come from families big in industry and politics.

Huber/Borchi

Pushkar

Just 15 km (9 miles) north of Ajmer, Pushkar is the holiest Hindu city in Rajasthan. According to legend, its lake was formed by a lotus flower falling from Brahma's hand, and bathing in its waters washed away all sins. The shores of the lake are lined with a number of *ghats* leading down to the water from where there's an almost continuous stream of pilgrims seeking purification.

Inevitably, such a major religious site attracted an enormous amount of temple building, but all the ancient ones were destroyed by the Moghul emperor Aurangzeb in the late 17th century. Only the big **Brahma Temple**, with a its four-headed sculpture of the god, predates them (14th century). Over the entrance is a *hans*, Brahma's goose symbol.

The **Savitri Temple**, honouring Brahma's wife, is on top of a hill an hour's walk southwest of town. It affords superb views, best enjoyed at sunrise and sunset.

Camel Fair

Pushkar's great fair is held in late October or November. With its traders, puppeteers, dancers, musicians and, of course, thousands of camels brought here to be bought and sold, it's an experience not to be missed. Try to turn up a few days before the official start of the fair, as often the most spectacular part is seeing the beasts arrive en masse.

Ranthambore

In the east of Rajasthan, not far from its border with the state of Madhya Pradesh, this area of unspoiled jungle was once the private hunting ground of the Maharajas of Jaipur. The huntsmen's favoured target was the equally regal tiger. In fact tiger hunting was not banned until 1970, and three years later Project Tiger was launched with the aim of preserving the few animals left. Since then the authorities displaced many of the villagers to the exterior of the park, not without meeting a certain opposition.

Today there are thought to be around 40 tigers in the **Ranthambore National Park**, along with leopards, hyenas, sloth bears, chital (spotted deer), sambar (the largest species of deer in India), wild boar and nilgai, a stately-looking antelope better known as the bluebull. Crocodiles flourish, and there's a superb variety of birds. Entrance to the park is restricted. You can only get there by making a reservation with the authorities, by jeep or in a 20-seater van called a canter. Their number is strictly limited. All of these are open vehicles — great for taking photos, but a little nerve-wracking should you actually have a

Robert Rybnikar

Breakfast is prepared over camel-dung fires at the traders' camp.

brief encounter with a tiger. They are also very cold in winter — bring plenty of warm clothes.

There is no guarantee that you will spot a tiger, but the other wildlife and scenery will be more than enough to compensate. The terrain is a combination of dense jungle and upland savannah, and at its centre is a large outcrop of rock with well-preserved remains of the 10th-century **Ranthambore Fort** on top. Founded by the Jat dynasty, it was conquered by Akbar in 1559, and came under the sway of Jaipur a century later.

Sanganer is known for its block- and screen-printed cotton fabrics.

Renata Holzbachová

Jaipur

The three cities of Jaipur, Delhi and Agra form India's "golden triangle", but whereas Delhi boasts 3,000 years of history, Jaipur is a virtual newcomer, less than 300 years old.

Jai Singh II (1688–1743) was chief of the Rajput Kachwaha clan, who ruled several kingdoms and princely states. In the 1720s, he took advantage of good relations with the Moghul ruler to abandon his fortress in Amber and found a new capital a few miles away on the plain. Work began in November 1727, and it took seven years to finish most of the construction. For the first time, a Rajput town was designed according to the principles of city planning laid down by ancient Hindu texts on architecture, with nine rectangular plots (symbolizing the nine divisions of the universe) separated by wide avenues intersecting at right angles. In the centre, the palace covered two plots. The new city was protected by a crenellated rampart 10 km (6 miles) in circumference, with 11 gates, and fortresses in the surrounding hills.

A distinguished warrior, Jai Singh was also passionately interested in art and astronomy. He preferred peace to war and dreamt of making Jaipur the capital of a unified Rajputana. His ambition was fulfilled, but only much later, when in 1948–49 the 22 Rajput States agreed to become part of a united India and to form one state, Rajasthan. Jaipur became the administrative and economic capital and is now at the head of a region of 342,000 sq km (132,000 sq miles) and nearly 70 million inhabitants.

The modern town of Jaipur, with a population of 3 million, has spread well beyond its original boundary, but within the fortifications, the layout of the old town and its buildings is virtually unchanged.

Pink City

Apart from the noise and the dust, the streets of Jaipur have nothing in common with the streets in other northern cities. They are spacious—up to 36 m (nearly 120 ft) wide—and the orange and pink-fronted houses are among India's most beautiful. A symbol of welcome, the colour pink was chosen in 1876 for the visit of the future King Edward VII, and ever since then, the owners have been obliged to conform and to repaint the façades regularly—a degree of uniformity contrary to Indian custom. But Jaipur begs to differ: when the town was founded, Jai Singh offered permits to numerous merchants and craftsmen, but only on condition that they used designated building materials.

Their descendants occupy the liveliest streets and markets in the city, where pedestrians jostle for space along with auto-rickshaws, camel-drawn carts, cars and vans. **Bapu** and **Nehru Bazaars** are devoted mainly to textiles, shoes and perfumes, **Tripolia Bazaar** to carvings, brassware and lacquer bracelets, and **Chandpol Bazaar** to carpets, trinkets and souvenirs. Each quarter of the town has its own "guild": near the Palace of the Winds, **Johari Bazaar** is the jewellers' quarter, which they share with sari sellers.

City Palace

Some of the palace apartments are still occupied by the descendants of the maharajahs, but the rest, with an architecture blending Moghul and Rajasthani styles, has been converted into a museum. You reach it by one of the two gateways, **Virendra Pol** or **Udai Pol**. The first opens onto a vast courtyard in the centre of which is the **Mubarak Mahal** (Palace of Welcome), designed to accommodate important guests. This attractive pavilion is used to display mostly costumes of the old maharajahs.

At the back of the courtyard, a staircase climbs to a **museum of weapons** displaying bows, daggers and other Moghul sabres. Pass through the splendid **Rajendra Pol**, a sculpted marble doorway framed by elephants, to reach a second courtyard with the **Diwan-i-Khas**, Audience Hall, in the centre, where you can see the two giant silver jars used by Maharaja Madho Singh II to carry a supply of Ganges water for his personal use during a visit to England in 1901.

On the north side, a third courtyard is adorned with four splendid doors representing the four seasons, the loveliest covered with polychrome peacocks. You

Recycling the *haveli*. The maharajas and prosperous merchants of Rajasthan often designed their *haveli* to be modest in their exterior appearance. However, they lavished their wealth on the interior, with immense courtyards, richly decorated walls. They can have five, six or even seven storeys. The exquisite ornamentation in sculpted stone evokes infinite trellises with inventive patterns. Many of these palaces have been abandoned or transformed into boutiques or hotels. This is the case in Jaipur for the Raj Palace and the Samode Haveli. You may find wood panels or old barred windowframes in the antique shops of the region, sometimes transformed into coffee table tops.

THE LAST MAHARAJAH

The Rajputs ruled the region for a good thousand years. In 1947, the creation of a democratic India put an end to their power. To encourage them to integrate in a united India, the government offered them various privileges, including an annual pension. But in 1971, Indira Gandhi abolished these privileges, and many maharajahs have since been forced to open their palaces to the public in order to pay for the upkeep.

In Jaipur, **Rambagh Palace** has not escaped this economic necessity. The luxurious residence, now converted into a hotel, was the home of the last Maharajah of Jaipur, Man Singh II, and his third wife Gayatri Devi. The couple had a colossal fortune and an extravagant lifestyle: the roads were closed to traffic an hour before they went out by car so that there would be no dust in the air, and their water was brought every morning from a special spring by four servants and a soldier. The couple ceased to rule over the town in 1949 but lost nothing of their popularity with the locals. In fact, when the Maharani Devi stood for the regional legislative elections against the Congress Party in 1962, she smashed all the records ever obtained by the opposition. Man Singh II died accidentally in England in 1970 in a polo match. His descendants still live in private apartments within the City Palace.

Tony McCombs

can also visit the **Diwan-i-Am**, the Audience Room where dignitaries and ambassadors were received. The royal thrones are displayed there.

The maharajah's private apartments can be partly visited on a special and quite costly guided tour called Royal Grandeur Tour.

Jantar Mantar

This huge observatory open to the sky (its name means "measuring instruments") was created by Jai Singh II around 1730. The maharajah was fascinated by astronomy and built five observatories in all, the one in Delhi being the first ever established in India (1724). Three others were set up at Ujjain, Varanasi and Mathura when Jai Singh became governor of Agra. The Mathura observatory has been destroyed, and of the survivors, that of Jaipur is the most impressive. Jai Singh kept himself informed of the work of Kepler, Galileo, Cassini and Newton, and made enquiries about the latest European discoveries before equipping the site.

The Jaipur observatory consists of a multitude of measuring instruments of monumental size, resembling a group of abstract scuptures. In reality, these are serious scientific instruments capable of accurately recording the position of the earth and other astronomical phenomena. Samrat Yantra, the giant sun dial, with a gnomon 27 m (88 ft) high, is the world's most accurate: it is graduated in 2-second intervals and the shadow moves the width of a hand every minute. Several of the instruments are designed to measure time, others to calculate eclipses or azimuths. The signs of the zodiac are also represented. Astrology has a strong influence on Hindu life, intervening for example, in the choice of a spouse and the propitious time for a wedding.

Hawa Mahal, Palace of the Winds

Built in 1799, the Palace of the Winds is one of Jaipur's great attractions. Situated in the heart of the old city, it is part of the City Palace complex. In very unusual style, it is five storeys high but has a depth of only a few yards. Its dark pink sandstone façade pierced by countless latticework windows set in three-sided bays indicate its original function, which was to allow the ladies of the harem to watch street life and processions while remaining discreetly hidden from public view. The building was designed with natural air conditioning. From the top there is a fine view over Jaipur.

Nahargarh Fort

The Tiger Fort, on a high ridge 6 km (4 miles) northwest side of

Jaipur, can be reached on foot. It is floodlit at night and famed for its exceptional setting and the views over the city and the Water Palace. Jai Singh had the fortress built in 1734 to protect the town, and cannon were fired to announce the time of day to everyone within hearing distance.

Gaitor

The cenotaphs *(chhatri)* of the maharajahs of Jaipur are grouped on this site below Nahagarh fort. They are lavishly sculpted in white marble with scenes of hunting and elephant battles.

Modern Town

Outside the ramparts, the new town stretches southwest of the old city.

Beyond the New Gate stretch the **Ram Niwas Gardens**. Designed in the middle of the 19th century, the garden includes a zoo specializing in breeding crocodiles, the **Ravindra Rangmanch Theatre**, a museum of modern art, and the imposing **Albert Hall**. This houses the collections of the Municipal Museum. Built in 1876 for the visit of the Prince of Wales, it has hardly changed since then. It displays a fine collection of ceramics, weapons, brassware and woodcarvings, all in all a good illustration of the Indian craftsmen's savoir-faire at the end of the 19th century.

A short drive south, following boulevard Jawaharlal Nehru, do not miss the temple of **Birla Mandir** (or Sri Lakshmi Narayan) in white marble. Its group of sculptures cover the entire panoply of Hindu deities, but there are also unusual representations of Christ, Moses, Confucius and Zarathustra! Only Muhammad is missing, it is forbidden to depict him in images.

Two lively temples. The inhabitants of Jaipur come every day to the **Govinda Deva Temple**, near the City Palace, to participate in *puja* (prayers and offerings). This sanctuary is dedicated to the blue-skinned god Krishna, eighth avatar of Vishnu. Govinda is the name that Krishna bore when he was a shepherd. The little **Ganesh Temple**, near Moti Dungri in the west part of town, is almost as busy, especially on Wednesdays, the day specially devoted to the elephant-headed god. The *puja* take place seven times a day (four times in the morning, three in the afternoon), and each time the god appears in different clothes. The prayers at the end of the afternoon are the most fervent of Hindu worship.

Clay Enos

Painted with thousands of flowers, the entrance to Amber fortress is dedicated to Ganesh.

Amber

The history of the Kachwaha princes begins in Amber, a colossal fortress 10 km (6 miles) from the Pink City that was their stronghold for seven centuries. On the way, at the northern exist of Jaipur, you pass the **Jal Mahal** or Water Palace (1799) standing in the middle of Lake Man Sagar.

The Fort

From afar, Amber's towers and pavilions, crowning the defensive walls built on vertiginous cliffs, look like a delicately coloured tiered cake coated in honey. Occupying the whole promontory, the 16th-century fort looms over the plain, its huge outline reflected in the shimmering waters of Lake Maota Sagar. You can get there on foot, in a jeep or on an elephant.

The Rajput princes who built the fort, the Kachwaha, claim to be descendants of the sun. But the richness of Amber owes more to historical fact than to legend. The first Rajput clan to have tied links with the Moghul emperors, the rulers of this area saw their wealth and influence increase as the power of the empire grew. Moghul taste thus infiltrated the architecture of Amber.

Suraj Pol, the Sun Gate, leads to an inner courtyard where you see the **Diwan-i-Am** (Hall of Public Audience) built on a huge terrace of white marble. The elegance of its red sandstone and white marble columns, with elephant-head capitals, was more than a match for any of the Moghul forts, to the point that the Emperor Jahangir took offence. To avoid any trouble, the columns were covered with stucco. But the splendour of Amber remained in secret: past the grandiose **Ganesh Pol**, giving access to the private apartments, the **Shish Mahal** (Palace of Mirrors), is lined with mirrors from floor to ceiling, glittering like a palace from *The Arabian Nights*. The **Jal Mandir** (Hall of Victory) and **Diwan-i-Khas** (Hall of Private Audience) are similarly resplendent. The **Sukh Niwas** (Hall of Pleasures) was fitted with an ingenious system of ventilation, with rose-water filling the air with fragrance, ending in the fountains of the garden courtyard. Everywhere, the polished marble still sparkles with the ancient opulence of the Kachwahas.

The **Man Singh Palace** (1599) was the ladies' quarters, where each of the 12 wives of the maharajah lived in her own apartments. They met in the communal salon of the elegant central **Baradari Pavilion**.

Down from the fort, the Hindu **Jagat Shiromani Temple**, dedicated to Krishna, is entered via a handsome door framed by elephants. The shrine dates from the 16th–17th centuries and has a remarkable group of bas-reliefs and sculpture.

A renowned textile company opened the **Anokhi Museum of Hand Printing** at Kheri Gate. It illustrates the traditional technique of woodblock printing. Demonstrations are given upstairs.

Jaigarh

Right next to Amber, this imposing fort perched on the heights still looks impregnable. Jai Singh had it built to replace an earlier position in 1726, in order to repulse attacks that might come from the east. It underwent a number of expansions, as attested by the many encircling walls. From the top, there's a magnificent view over the fort of Amber down below the plain, Jaipur and Jal Mahal.

A steep half-hour walk from Amber, Jaigarh has several points of interest. In the 18th-century **foundry**, for example, you can see how the barrels of cannon were cast and bored, while the armoury has a large collection of swords and other implements used in warfare, but the most interesting aspect is the residential district, with the Garden Palace superbly looming over a void, around a Persian garden planted with mango trees. Local inhabitants organize puppet shows.

At the eastern end of the fort, the **Jaivana**, a cannon 6 m (20 ft) long and weighing 50 tonnes, was cast at the Jaigarh foundry in 1720 on the orders of Jai Singh. One of the largest cannons in the world, it has only been fired once, a trial shot said to have sent a cannonball a distance of 38 km (23 miles)!

Sanganer

Paper-making, block- and screen-printing are the specialities of Sanganer, a town 10 km (6 miles) south of Jaipur. The technique of using carved teak blocks to print designs on textiles has been practised here for at least 500 years. Several thousands of craftsmen work together: wood-carvers, printers and manufacturers of dyes, natural and artificial. Every design requires several wood blocks—one for the outline of the pattern, and one for each colour. The printer presses his teak block onto a sponge soaked in paint, then applies it onto the fabric with remarkable precision, square after square.

Blue pottery. Man Singh I, supreme commander of the armies of Emperor Akbar in the 16th century, became an enthusiast of Turco-Persian pottery. He invited many Moghul craftsmen to settle in the region. You can see their descendants at work, notably in the **Kripal Kumbh workshop** on Shiva Marg, to the west of the Pink City, or in **Sanganer,** 10 km (6 miles) away. There is no clay in the Jaipur region; its famous pottery is made from a mixture of earth and gum. It is shaped by hand and fired only once. The Persian motifs and floral ornamentation use turquoise blues obtained from copper sulphate and dark blues from cobalt oxide. Artists have introduced a wider range of colours nowadays.

You'll easily spot the printing shops by the quantities of tablecloths, saris and bedspreads drying outside their doors. Three days of exposure to the sun and rinsing in the waters of Aman-i-Shah river fixes the colours permanently. They should not lose their brilliance, even after washing in hot water.

The Road to Agra

The loaded camels you may see on the road from Jaipur to Agra do nothing to relieve the monotony of the landscape. However, it is well worth stopping to visit Keoladeo National Park at Bharatpur, 42 km (26 miles) west of Agra, and the town of Fatehpur Sikri, former capital of the Moghul empire.

Keoladeo National Park

The ideal period to explore this bird sanctuary—one of the largest in the world—is from November to February. Also known as the **Bharatpur Reserve,** the park consists of artificially flooded zones created by the local maharajah in 1902 for duck-shooting parties. British viceroys and foreign royalty used to indulge in orgies of killing. Today hunting is banned.

Apart from the resident birdlife (over 350 species), thousands of migratory species can be seen here at the right season: herons, pelicans, marabou storks, egrets and cormorants, and from January to March a flock of Siberian cranes winters in the park. In the woodland you may see spotted deer and nilghai antelope. Towards noon, sinister pythons—non-venomous, they kill their prey by suffocation—slither out of the foliage to curl up in the sun. You can get around the reserve by cart, cycle-rickshaw or bicycle.

Fatehpur Sikri

In the mid-16th century, the Moghul emperor Akbar fled court gossip to visit a hermit, Salim Chisti. This ascetic lived in a cave on a mountain named Sikri, 35 km (22 miles) from Agra. He prophesied that Akbar, who up to then had remained childless despite having 300 wives, would soon have an heir. The prediction came true, and the emperor immediately decided to found the most grandiose capital of the Moghul empire right there on Mount Sikri: Fatehpur, the City of Victory. An Englishman, Ralph Finch wrote in 1585: "Its streets are not so beautiful as the streets of Agra, but the City is bigger and its population very numerous (…). Agra and Fatehpur are both bigger and more populous than London." According to the same source, Akbar had a reserve for snow leopards, tigers, falcons and tame deer. Abandoned only 15 years after being built because of political unrest and a lack of water, Fatehpur Sikri became a ghost town. Nothing remains of the hundreds of houses that once covered its slopes, but inside the walls, the red sandstone palaces have withstood the centuries.

Hindus, Muslims and Jesuits lived together at the court. Akbar, passionately interested in religion, developed a new cult called Deen Ilahi, which tried to blend together the principal religious groups. Akbar's desire for syncretism exploded in the architecture, where Indian, Persian and even European influences can be seen side by side. Amidst luxuriant vegetation, wild gardens and red bougainvillaea, one palace follows the next in a jumble of columns, pools, pavilions, domes and airy summerhouses designed for long hot evenings.

The sovereign resided in **Jodh Bai Palace**. His harem lived around him, and a room with stone latticework allowed the ladies to see without being seen. Near the Diwan-i-Am, in the "games courtyard", the ground is marked out like a giant chequerboard where Akbar played *pachisi*, the national game similar to ludo, using young slaves to represent the pieces. The white marble tomb of the hermit Salim Chisti dominates the courtyard of the mosque, southwest of the palace.

A poem in white marble, the Taj Mahal
changes colours with the light.

Agra

For almost 150 years, Agra was the capital of the Moghul Empire. Its monuments testify to the wealth and splendour of a state which covered a large part of India during the 16th and 17th centuries. The court at Agra inspired the most prodigious stories all across Europe. It was recounted that dishes of rice were garnished with sheets of gold leaf, that twice a year the people were given a gift equivalent to the emperor's weight in silver, and even that the fish in the fountains wore golden nose-rings.

The extravagance of the court was reflected all over the city. The emperors were patrons of the arts, and their lavishness made the fortunes of many a craftsman living outside the fort. The town became an important trading centre, and when the capital was removed to Delhi, some 200 km (125 miles) away, the court left behind a rich and famous city, which attracted hordes of travellers even in the 17th century.

Today, Agra looks like a large provincial town. Widespread, crossed by wide avenues, it is an airy city, though quite dirty, and it's difficult to believe that the population exceeds 1.7 inhabitants. The peace is disturbed only by the rickshaw and auto-rickshaw drivers, constantly harassing the tourists.

Like Delhi, Agra has an old town next to the more recent areas known as the Cantonment (a reminder of the British presence), where most of the Western-style hotels are located.

Red Fort

The emperors Akbar, Jahangir and Shah Jahan all ruled from this stronghold. Akbar had it built by the banks of the Yamuna between 1567 and 1575, on the ruins of a Hindu edifice. The original plain and simple military building was gradually transformed into a magnificent palace, to which each emperor added something typical of the creative genius of his era.

The high red sandstone ramparts are reminiscent of the walls of Delhi's Red Fort, built later by Shah Jahan. However, the architecture of the two constructions illustrates two very different stories. Whereas in the Delhi fort, Islamic symmetry and form evoke the rigorous structure of society under Shah Jahan, the varied styles displayed in Agra's architecture are a reflection of the open-mindedness of Akbar. To the right of the access ramp , past the **Amar Singh Gate**, you reach **Jahangiri Mahal**, the palace built for Akbar's son, blending Persian and Indian influences. The central courtyard is adorned with intricate geometrical patterns and birds typical of the Indian iconography, a far cry from the Delhi buildings, where Shah Jahan respected Islamic law to the letter and forbade any representation of living creatures, human or animal.

Largely modified under Shah Jahan, the fort has kept the superb **Moti Masjid** (Pearl Mosque), unfortunately closed to the public, and **Khas Mahal**, its walls clad with white marble. It is prolonged by the elegant **Musamman Burj** (Octagonal Tower), with affords a magnificent view over the Yamuna River and the Taj Mahal. Shah Jahan was to die there after eight years of captivity in 1666, having been overthrown by his son. You can also visit the **Shish Mahal**, its walls encrusted with mirrors, and the **Diwan-i-Khas**, the private audience hall of Shah Jahan. Past the **Macchi Bhavan**, surrounded by an arched gallery, near the **Nagina Masjid** (Jewel Mosque), the **Diwan-i-Am** was reserved for public hearings. It is not in marble, as you might think, but in red sandstone covered with plaster.

Around the Jama Masjid

In this part of town, a few minutes from the fort, the descendants of the first Moghul craftsmen are still at work. As in most of the old towns of northern India, narrow streets lined with shops are home to a host of tradesmen, grouped according to

Marble inlay. Grouped in the Nai ki Mandi district, the craftsmen skilled in the art of *pietra dura* — inlaid stone — work in teams under the leadership of the workshop head. The white marble is brought from the Markana quarries in Rajasthan. Semi-precious stones come from all over the world, and the Indian Ocean supplies shells in hues of green and purple. A thin orange-coloured coating is applied to the marble to facilitate the engraving. Once carved, the marble is polished back to its initial whiteness. The semi-precious stones are roughly cut with a bandsaw, then finely chiselled into strips. A hand-powered lathe is used to file them to the required shapes and sizes. The stones are then fitted into the marble like pieces of a jigsaw puzzle, and set with a glue whose composition is kept secret. The time required to make each object is considerable: three months for the lid of a small box; six months for an inlaid tray.

Lian Chang

their trade. Spice merchants here, kite-makers, sari sellers or jewellers there; further along are the toolmakers, weavers and wedding specialists. The dhurrie sellers have the monopoly in the **Kinari Bazaar** on the main street. Around the mosque, cafés offer a limited menu of spicy dishes swimming in oil; customers sip sweet, milky tea far from the madding crowd of tourists.

The **Jama Masjid**, or Friday Mosque, with its striped red and white dome, is squeezed in among the houses in the heart of this old quarter of town. It was built by Shah Jahan in 1648, in honour of his favourite daughter, Jahanara.

Northwest of the mosque and on the other side of Hing ki Mandi Road, the **Nai ki Mandi** district harbours the tiny shoemakers' shops and the workshops of the marble-inlayers, who ply their trade exactly as they did three centuries ago. In the 1970s, there were still 15,000 of them working in the backyards of the old town. But the trade has fallen on hard times and their numbers have greatly dwindled.

The *pietra dura* technique was used to decorate the walls of Taj Mahal. | The Red Fort in Agra is still occupied in part by the Indian army. | A snake charmer near Jama Masjid.

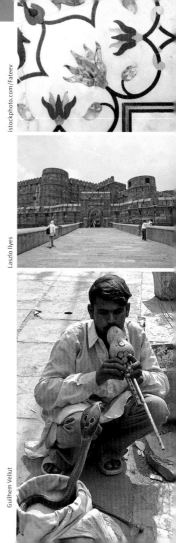

Taj Mahal

Shah Jahan dedicated the Taj Mahal to the memory of his favourite wife, Mumtaz Mahal, who died in 1631 after 17 years of marriage, while giving birth to their 14th child. In his despair, the emperor threw all his grief and energy into creating a mausoleum that would surpass in beauty all the other wonders of the world. The work took 22 years and 20,000 workers.

Within the octagonal chamber are the empty tombs of Mumtaz and Shah Jahan. The real tombs are in the basement.

"An absolutely perfect pearl against a background of azure" was how the artist William Hodges described it in 1876. The Taj Mahal's impressive size, its balanced proportions, its setting in an exquisite garden of perfect symmetry, and its dazzling white marble have made it an exceptional monument. Even the crowds of visitors don't disturb the almost solemn atmosphere it creates. The play of light at different times makes it pass from mauve to ivory to pearl grey or gold.

The Buildings

Moghul architecture flourished in India under Shah Jahan. It is said that the architect of the Taj Mahal was inspired by the Omeyyades Mosque in Damascus, the tomb of Tamerlane in Samarkand and the mausoleums of Humayun and Khan Khanan in Delhi. However, he borrowed only the elements that were the most appropriate. For example, he placed second-

A mysterious architect. The mystery surrounding the identity of the architect of the Taj Mahal has inspired many a legend. It is said that Shah Jahan had the unfortunate man's eyes put out once the mausoleum was finished, so that he could never build anything as beautiful again. Another version recounts that the architect was unable to think up a design capable of expressing the emperor's sorrow, so the emperor had the architect's wife put to death. Overcome by grief, the master builder was finally able to undertake his mission. These stories arise from a real and even more disturbing enigma: no one really knows who drew up the plans of the Taj Mahal. Certain authors name a Venetian called Verronea, though local accounts make no mention of a European. Many names have been suggested over the centuries, but contemporary documents contradict each other and many are simply fake. The hypothesis judged today to be the most probable is that the mysterious architect was none other than the emperor himself.

ary buildings and decorative minarets on each side of the Taj Mahal to temper the severity of one single edifice. To preserve the essential symmetry of the whole, he built a counterpart mosque next to the mausoleum, although the new building could never be a holy place as it was incorrectly oriented in relation to Mecca.

The Taj Mahal is the greatest achievement of Indo-Islamic architecture. Numerous elements of Indian inspiration distinguish it from true Muslim architecture inherited from Persia. For instance, Hindus often carved their temples from rock and left only a tiny space in the interior. This influence is also shown in the Taj Mahal: its outside proportions are as impressive as the interior spaces are narrow and few. The cupola is closed underneath and is therefore neither accessible nor of any practical use. The mausoleum, like many other Moghul monuments, is like a huge sculpture.

The Gardens
For the Moghuls, a tomb wasn't only designed to preserve the memory of the defunct, but also to act as his or her dwelling. Thus, it was always placed in a garden, which the ruler would have landscaped during his lifetime and where he would hold receptions. After his death, his

Three fine views of the Taj. There are not many hills around Agra, and not many view points for taking your photos of the Taj Mahal. The **Red Fort** is the ideal place for a first glimpse. From a distance, the tomb has a particular beauty arising from its size, shape and whiteness. The architectural details are suddenly revealed from the **gardens** surrounding it: stand in front of it and you will see it mirrored in the pool along an axis of perfect symmetry. To the east of the mausoleum, a narrow path leads to the edge of the Yamuna. For a few dozen rupees, a small boat will take you to the **opposite bank of the river**. The surroundings are quiet and the view sublime.

court and hundreds of servants would continue to surround him.

The tomb of Mumtaz was the centre of a ceremony which went way beyond the norm. Musicians and poets endlessly sang her praises.

On the west side of the gardens, a small museum presents documents and souvenirs relating to the time of the Taj Mahal's design.

Across the Yamuna
An auto-rickshaw ride across the Agra Bridge is delightful, and

The ceiling of Akbar's Tomb at Sikandra.

from **Mehtab Bagh** on the other side of the river there is a lovely view of the Taj Mahal. It is said that Shah Jahan had originally planned to build an identical mausoleum for himself in black marble on the left bank of the river, and that a bridge was to have linked the two. You can also take a boat across.

Itimad-ud-Daulah

The father of the Persian poetess Noor Jahan, wife of the Emperor Jahangir, rests in a mausoleum on the other side of the Yamuna. Noor Jahan had his tomb built in 1622; it was the first structure in India to incorporate the technique of *pietra dura*, brought from Italy: white marble inlaid with coloured stones representing flowers, trees, fruit, animals, birds, wine jars and even people. Smaller than the Taj, and attracting fewer visitors, the tomb is a gem, with beautiful marble lat-

ticework letting in the light. The garden is alive with ground squirrels and monkeys.

Ram Bagh

About 5 km (3 miles) northeast of the Taj Mahal, Ram Bagh was laid out on the banks of the river in 1528 by Babar, the first emperor of the Moghul dynasty, who was largely inspired by the Persian tradition of gardens. With raised walkways that would be covered with carpets, water channels and cascades, it represents the Islamic ideal of paradise.

Akbar's Tomb

Sikandra, a town some 12 km (7 miles) north of Agra, is the site of Akbar's Tomb. Built of red sandstone inlaid with white marble, it lies in the middle of a vast park overrun with monkeys, peacocks and deer. Heralded by an enormous *iwan* (door) flanked by four three-storey minarets, the mausoleum was built during Akbar's lifetime but demanded so many modifications that he died before it was finished. The structure is of interest as it demonstrates Akbar's desire to combine the features he preferred in Muslim, Hindu and Buddhist architecture.

A short distance from there you can se the tomb of his favourite wife, Mariam Zamani, the mother of Jahangir.

ANIMALS ABOUT TOWN

It isn't unusual to come face to face with a **dromedary** harnessed to a cart in the cluttered streets of Jaipur or wending its way through Delhi's thoroughfares. With its lacklustre coat and sad eyes, the urban dromedary bears little resemblance to its majestic cousin of the Thar Desert. The camel fair at Pushkar is held in November. Thousands of camels are bought and sold and camel races are organized.

Indians have great respect for **elephants**, admiring them for their strength and the wisdom, knowledge and good fortune that they symbolize. Ganesh, the elephant-headed god, is one of the most popular in the Hindu pantheon. India has some 20,000 elephants, and Hindu art is permeated with images to their glory. The princes of Amber were particularly fond of these gentle giants who carried them around in majesty. Nowadays, some 50 beasts carry tourists to the gates of the fortress. Working on a shift system, they are members of a "trade union" placed under government control. An elephant festival takes place in March in Jaipur.

You'll see two types of **monkey** in Northern India. The aggressive rhesus monkey, with a brown head and bright red backside, is the most common. The long-tailed langur, with beetling black eyebrows, black ears, face, feet and hands and a grey pelt, is bigger but more gentle. Langurs have occupied the fortress at Amber since the days of the maharajahs, living in total freedom under the guardianship of a state employee. The association which takes care of their food supply brings fruit by rickshaw from Jaipur every morning. When numbers become too large, some are transferred to the Sariska Game Park 120 km (75 miles) away along the Delhi road. In Jaipur, dozens of monkeys live around the Galtaji Hanuman Temple. A priest distributes sacks of bananas every day between 4 and 5 p.m.

Norma Cornes

The Jain sculptures, carved directly in the rock face, measure up to 17 m (56 ft) high.

Paul Kennes

Madhya Pradesh

When Kipling chose Madhya Pradesh as the setting for The Jungle Book, *the state was rich in thick forests and wild beasts of all descriptions. And to a certain extent, it still is.*

The wild beasts of the jungle have paid dearly for the passion for hunting shown in turn by local princes, the Moghuls and the British. The palace museum, in Gwalior, Jai Vilas, is full of moth-eaten stuffed tigers, the trophies of ancient maharajahs. These big cats would most certainly have disappeared from the region if various conservation organizations had not intervened. Project Tiger, launched in 1973, is supported by the World Wide Fund for Nature (WWF) and is also effective in Rajasthan. Today, the territory of Madhya Pradesh encompasses more than 25 nature reserves (jungle and savannah), the biggest of which reach about 2,000 sq km (770 sq miles) in area. Only a few harbour tigers and leopards.

For centuries, the region was the theatre not only of struggle between man and beast, but of ceaseless conflicts between local rulers and Hindu or Muslim invaders. Many dynasties have come and gone. But unlike other states, northern Madhya Pradesh still retains handsome vestiges of Hindu architecture. The conical temples of Gwalior, Orchha and Khajuraho were spared the destructive frenzy that characterized the Muslim invasions.

Gwalior

So many dynasties and so many maharajahs have occupied the throne of Gwalior that the history of its thousand-year-old fort is an inextricable tangle of characters, intrigues and bloodbaths, with the leading roles played by the Moghuls and the British. Gwalior fort remains associated with the most tragic events of the Indian Mutiny. It was here that the revolt was finally put down.

Huddled at the foot of the imposing citadel, to the north and northeast, the old town of modest markets and earthen roads enjoys a new-found tranquillity. Lashkar (The Camp), founded in 1809, is the new town. It is spreading inexorably towards the horizon, and its population will soon number a million.

Gwalior Fort

Overlooking the town from a height of 100 m (330 ft), the citadel occupies the entire hill. Most of its palaces and other buildings were constructed by Man Singh, a prince of the Tomara dynasty, which came to power towards the end of the 14th century. Thanks to its formidable ramparts more than

PHOOLAN DEVI, BANDIT QUEEN

A political figure who took up the cause of the Untouchables, and a national heroine known in India as the "Bandit Queen", Phoolan Devi is also the quasi-mythical leading character in a film which has enjoyed international success. But the Chambal Valley, between Agra and Gwalior, still trembles at the memory of the 55 killings she carried out there. Long before she appeared on television as a neat little woman in an impeccable sari, Phoolan Devi was the leader of the Dacoits, armed bandits who live in the forests of northern Madhya Pradesh and terrorize the local population.

Born into a low caste and married when 11 to a man over 20 years her senior (in exchange for a cow), raped by police and by landowners, Phoolan Devi fell into the hands of the Dacoits and under the spell of their desire for vengeance against India's inegalitarian society. She became their most fervent and most feared member. Her spectacular arrest before the cameras of Indian television began her notoriety. A sentence of 11 years imprisonment turned her into a living legend. After her release, Phoolan Devi learned to read and write, married and served as a member of the Indian parliament.

Threatened by further imprisonment in 1997, she returned into hiding. She was shot dead by masked gunmen in 2001.

3 km (2 miles) in length, this long remained one of India's most impregnable strongholds. In places, the cliff has been steepened to make it unscaleable, in others it overhangs. However, all this was not enough to prevent Man Singh, who ruled from 1486, from being killed 30 years later when the Lodi sovereigns of Delhi laid siege to his citadel.

Jain Sculptures

You reach the gates of the fort by the south or northwest of the hill. Amazing giant figures carved out of the rock line the steep path. Sculpted in about 1450 by followers of the Jain religion, they are up to 17 m (56 ft) high. The largest and doubtless the most impressive of the groups of statuary lies to the south, stretching across almost a kilometre (half a mile) of rock wall.

Man Singh Palace

Also known as Chit Mandir, the grandiose palace has six domed towers. Construction was begun at the end of the 15th century, and its rather baroque appearance contrasts starkly with the sobriety of Moghul palaces. The Hindu influence is apparent in the colourful ducks, peacocks and elephants that decorate the walls of the first inner courtyard. Such images would be regarded as sacrilegious in a Muslim palace.

Bedrooms follow reception rooms and dressing rooms in a maze of galleries and corridors, some of which lead underneath the palace and emerge 10 km (6 miles) away. In the prayer room, the niches once framed statuettes of the gods. The public rooms—halls for dancing and music—all have latticed openings pierced high in the walls, to allow the ladies of the court to watch the proceedings without being seen. The lower vaults evoke the citadel's more tragic times: under

Sati and *jauhar*. In 1232, the eight widows of a Rajput prince who was defeated in battle were burnt alive beneath the Man Singh Palace. The practice of *sati* (individual), or *jauhar* (collective) was at first exclusively carried out by the wives of princes. When defeat seemed inevitable, the rajah donned his traditional costume and left to be killed in battle while the ladies of the harem went to the stake in order to avoid falling into the hands of the invaders. Later, wives of all ranks were cremated on the departed husband's funeral pyre, whether they agreed or not. The British put an end to *sati* in 1829, which didn't stop extremists from putting it into practise. The British also outlawed the murder of baby girls at birth.

the Moghuls, the room where Man Singh used to keep swings was reserved for hangings, and the basements became prisons.

Gujari Mahal

Of Man Singh's nine wives, his favourite, Mrignayani, was the daughter of a milkman and the only one not from a high caste. As the eight other wives refused to associate with her, Man Singh built a second palace for her alone, the Gujari Mahal. It now houses an Archaeological Museum with collections of antiquities together with Hindu and Jain sculpture.

Jahangiri Mahal

Other palaces occupy the middle of the fortress, though none is as well preserved as Man Singh Palace. The Karan Palace stands to the west, while the palaces of the Moghul Emperors Jahangir and Shah Jahan were built near Lake Jauhar Kund. Jahangiri Mahal is a blend of architectural styles and is profusely carved; it was used by the women of the royal household, and it was there that the eight widows committed *jauhar* in 1282.

Sasbahu Temples

Two temples, 1000 years old, stand on the east side of the hill. The king's mother-in-law built a shrine in honour of Vishnu, and his daughter-in-law dedicated hers to Shiva. Hindu in style, the buildings were desecrated by the Muslims, and many of their fine statuettes have lost their arms or face. From the promontory, you can see old Gwalior on your left, a military zone straight ahead and the wealthy modern sector to the right. An enormous Sikh temple built in 1954 and faced in white marble stands at the foot of the hill.

Teli Ka Mandir

This temple, 32 m (105 ft) high, was built in the 9th century on the occasion of a royal wedding. It is quite unlike Moghul mausoleums, Persian mosques or buildings of Western influence. Its heavy pyramidal form, thick walls and abundant carvings are characteristic of primitive Indian art. The new wife of the king was originally from South India, and the building copies the style of her homeland, as is clear from the small number of carvings on the outside walls. The temple was a monument with a didactic purpose: newly married, the royal couple were shut inside for three days with an instructor to teach them the pleasures of love. All over the inside walls, carved reliefs show the young couple dancing, kissing and making love. The last sculpture shows them raising a hand in farewell.

Old Town

A stroll through the streets of old Gwalior will bring you to the 17th-century mosque, the **Tomb of Tansen**—one of Emperor Akbar's famed musicians—and the **mausoleum of Muhammad Gaus**, a fine example of Moghul architecture.

Jai Vilas Mahal

In the modern town, this palace has been the property of the Scindia family since the days of British rule and was the fief of the last Maharajah of Gwalior. A replica of an Italian *palazzo*, it was built in 1874 and has more than 300 rooms. Certain wings have been turned into a museum, which houses a host of objects belonging to generations of maharajahs. There is a Rolls Royce, and a silver electric train set which used to bring round the liqueurs and cigars after dinner.

Durbar Hall, with crystal furniture and approached by a crystal staircase, has two huge chandeliers each measuring 12.5 m (41 ft) in diameter and weighing 3.5 tonnes. They were hung only after the resistance of the ceiling was tested by hauling ten elephants up on ropes.

Jhansi

Against a backdrop of craggy hills, green plantations and fields of mustard yellow gradually give way to rocks and a semi-desert landscape. Suddenly on the left, perched on a hill, a group of dazzlingly white Jain temples comes into view. Some 20 km (12 miles) before Jhansi, **Datia** is famous for its seven-storey palace. It has been abandoned but the pavilions and painted ceilings are well preserved. Right at the top, stone elephants sit in state.

H.R.H. Madhavrao Scindia. When he took Gwalior 200 years ago, Mahaji Scindia commanded an army of 100,000 sabres. His descendant, Madhavrao Scindia, son of the last Maharajah of Gwalior, born in 1945, retained the prestige of the title earned in those glorious days. His faithful subjects referred to him as "His Royal Highness", and throngs of secretaries and servants bowed when he passed or scattered him with rose petals. The inhabitants of Gwalior carried him to take his place in parliament at the age of 26, and when he died in an air crash in 2001—confirming the tendency of Gwalior's ruling family to die young—foot soldiers carried the palanquin bearing his body to the royal crematorium. Scindia, who campaigned for contraception, economic expansion and cricket, was Rajiv Gandhi's Minister for Tourism, Aviation and Railways. He was mourned by thousands.

Paul Kennes

Behind its rural aspect, Orchha hides an unexpected history and the ruins of numerous temples.

Jhansi is a transit town and seems at first no more than a tangle of crowded roads. The fort provides an interesting panoramic view of the region. Built in 1613 by Maharajah Bir Singh Deo, it was taken by the British, then given to the Scindia family in 1858. A colony of monkeys has invaded the ruins and the old British base. At the foot of the wall, a fresco depicts the battle during which the Rani of Jhansi was killed; she led the rebels, dressed as a soldier.

Orchha

On the road from Jhansi to Khajuraho, the serene village of Orchha is like something out of a fairy tale. The 16-km (10-mile) stretch between Jhansi and Orchha is enchanting. Expanses of water shimmer behind groves of dazzling green, and streams run through the peaceful landscape. The village itself is full of charm, its lanes lined with pink-painted houses, children playing in the streets, and forming a surreal backdrop, countless ruined temples rise up on the horizon, witness to a glorious past.

A powerful Rajput capital founded beside the river Betwa in 1531, Orchha became the leading city of the region under the Bundela dynasty (16th–17th centuries). It boasted no fewer than 45 temples for more than 70,000 inhabitants. Bir Singh Deo, who built the fortress of Jhansi, came to the throne in 1605. He was defeated in 1627 by the armies of Aurangzeb, who was only 9 years old at the time. Orchha enjoyed a flourishing 17th centur, but in 1783 lost its status as capital to the nearby town of Tikamgadh.

Temples and Palaces

In the village centre, a massive platform supports the **Chaturbhuj Temple**. King Madhukar, predecessor of Bir Singh Deo, had it built for Ganesh Kunwari with

LEGEND OF ORCHHA

The six wives of Madhukar, Maharajah of Orchha (1554–92), were all devotees of the cult of Krishna, with the exception of the Maharani Ganesh Kunvar. She worshipped Rama (the god Vishnu, who during his seventh visit to earth took on the appearance of a strong and courageous man). One day this princess refused to go on a pilgrimage to the birthplace of Krishna, preferring to visit the birthplace of her own god. The king gave his permission, on condition that she would bring Rama back home with her.

Ganesh arrived at the place where Rama was born, a thousand kilometres from Orchha, not far from Varanasi. Coming to a river bank, she sat down and prayed for several months, but the god remained silent. In desperation, she tried three times to throw herself into the river, but each time the current carried her back to the bank. Then she saw, a short distance away, a stone that began to move and to take on the shape of the divinity. When Ganesh explained her mission, the statue agreed to accompany her, but on three conditions: first, the Maharani should go home on foot carrying the stone god; second, once the statue was set down in Orchha it should never be moved; and third, Rama demanded to be revered as a king.

Hearing of these conditions, Madhukar hastened to build the temple of Chaturbhuj, where he planned to welcome the god. But Ganesh returned to Orchha before the temple was completed, so she placed Rama in her own palace, which she converted into a temple to comply with his wishes. To this day, the statue has never been moved, and two royal guards watch over it as if it were a king.

Carol Mitchell

the intention of placing the statue of Rama there. From the top of the steps of the spiral staircase, the temple offers a complete panorama of the surroundings, in particular the city and the other temples.

Nearby, **Ram Raja** glows with over-bright colours—yellow and salmon pink. This old palace is the busiest place of worship in Orchha.

Just west of the village, the temple of **Lakshimi Narayan** (1662) is a curiosity in itself. Bir Singh Deo had it made of moulded bricks, a building material usually kept for fortresses, and it was renovated by Prithvi Singh in 1793. Ceilings and walls are covered with well-preserved frescoes depicting the fort of Jhansi and animals of all kinds. There are some interesting battle scenes between British and Moghul forces. The military uniforms and life in the camps are shown in precise detail, and the British are shown in caricature, all sporting large curling moustaches.

Cross the Betwa to reach the **Raj Mahal**, one-time residence of Madhukar. It retains some fine wall paintings. A few hundred vultures live in the towers, and at dawn or dusk you'll probably see one of them setting off on its sinister rounds. The adjacent **Sheesh Mahal**, once accommodation for the king's guests, is now a hotel.

Four great national parks. The **Bandhavgarh** and **Kanha** reserves, in the centre of Madhya Pradesh, offer the best chance of spotting tiger, as well as a whole range of antelope, water buffalo, monkeys and porcupines. The bears and the leopards only emerge at night. Near to Gwalior or to Khajuraho, the **Madhav** park gives sanctuary to tigers, and crocodiles lie in wait in Lake Sakhya Sagar. Birdlovers flock to Keoladeo Park in Rajasthan, 55 km (34 miles) west of Agra.

Robert Rybnikar

Its upper floors offer an ideal vantage point for admiring the landscape. Below, the **Rai Praveen Mahal** bears the name of the poetess for whom it was built in 1676. Surrounded by a magnificent garden and equipped with an elaborate water-supply system, it was designed to make life pleasant for Rai Praveen. Further south, the *chhatri*, memorials to the kings of Orchha, lie by the river. Despite their somewhat dilapidated state, they are interesting to see.

Khajuraho

This is one of the best-known sites in the whole of the subcontinent. Its temples and their legendary erotic carvings by unknown craftsmen are one of the most recognizable images of India in the West—no doubt because this artistic celebration of life and its pleasures is so contrary to the values of the Old Testament. The erotic scenes, however, don't occupy more than ten per cent of the temple friezes. Scenes of hunting, work, battle, bathing, feasting, resting—indeed all aspects of life and love are also depicted.

Unlike the *Kama Sutra*—which celebrates "healthy" love-making—the temples display rather more daring images. The most astonishing is undoubtedly that of a man "engaged" with a horse, under the horrified gaze of his companions. Such scenes of zoophilia, although rare, are enough to raise questions about the origin and significance of the erotic carvings at Khajuraho. Could they simply be didactic illustrations of the *Kama Sutra*? Or are they images from Tantric

Paul Kennes

Famous the world over, the erotic sculptures of Khajuraho only represent a small portion of the temple friezes.

philosophy, which holds that sexual relations allow the soul to leave the body and attain the ultimate liberation, or *moksha*?

The temples were built by the Chandela kings in the 9th and 10th centuries. The architecture was inspired by ancient Hindu texts, according to which temples are a symbol of the indestructible universal order. For this reason, places of worship were given the appearance of monoliths by carving them out of the rock. Somewhere around the beginning of the second millennium, the architects found it more convenient to build with stone, while still remaining faithful to older techniques. The walls were made thick and solid and the empty spaces restricted. From an architectural viewpoint, the Hindu ideal is a sort of monolithic tower with a very cramped interior.

The design of the Khajuraho temples incorporates five essential elements: the porch opens onto an ante-room, which in turn gives onto the main hall. From there, a vestibule leads to a shrine sheltering the divinity. Some of the monuments are made of granite but mainly pink, ochre and pale yellow sandstone quarried at Panna was used. The entrances face east.

Of the original 85 temples, 25 have survived. They are distributed in three main groups, eastern, western and southern. Adjacent to modern Khajuraho, the western group, comprising eight temples, is considered the finest, and the southern the least interesting.

Western Group

Seven of the eight temples stand among flower beds within a park. Only **Matangesvara**, still in use, is outside the enclosure. It contains a lingam, the symbol of Shiva, which is 2.5 m (8.5 ft) high.

Dedicated to Shiva, **Kandariya Mahadeva** is the biggest shrine at Khajuraho, 31 m (102 ft) high, and the most successful from an architectural and artistic point of view. The scenes of its carved processional friezes are remarkable, with more than 200 statues inside and over 600 outside set in three bands: figures of gods, goddesses, musicians and erotic

groups. They are among the most explicit in Khajuraho and only slightly more modest than those of the neighbouring **Jagadamba** temple, which shares the same platform at the back of the park, along with the little **Mahadeva** temple.

The carvings are of admirable finesse and elegance. Each panel is about a metre (3 ft) long, some temples having up to 800 panels. The king is identified by his beard and by his richly caparisoned horse. Celestial nymphs, dancers and women in general are carved with particular delicacy.

The oldest temple of the group is **Lakshmana**, dating from about AD 950, richly carved and one of the best-preserved. A procession of elephants, horses, soldiers, acrobats and dancers parades around the basement; gods and goddesses, graceful nymphs, groups of lovers, ecstatic minstrels, battle and hunting scenes cover the sides.

The small **Varaha** temple contains a gigantic carved boar in highly polished sandstone dating from the early 10th century. He is one of the avatars of Vishnu, to whom the temple is dedicated.

In the northeast corner, a large statue of the bull Nandi, Shiva's mount, opposite the **Vishvanatha** temple, identifies it as a shrine to Shiva. The sculptures of women here are particularly evocative.

Eastern Group

At the edge of the old village, this group includes three beautifully sculpted Jain temples. **Parsvanatha**, the largest, is remarkable for the delicacy of the decoration—note the woman making up her eyes with kohl, another painting the soles of her feet, and one tying bells to her ankles.

Next to it, **Adinatha** houses a startling black image of the deity, the only Jain element in the building. Adinatha means First Lord, he was the first of the *tirthankara*, the ancient Jain masters

Shantinatha is a relatively modern shrine containing antique pieces including a statue of Adinatha 4.5 m (15 ft) tall.

Within the enclosure, the **Jain Museum** is a circular gallery displaying statues of 24 *tirthankara*.

Brian Gratwicke

Crested serpent eagle *(Spilornis cheela)* in Panna National Park.

Old Village

After more than 500 years of power, the Chandela had to surrender to the Moghuls, and their capital Khajuraho sank into obscurity as a remote village. Today it has no more than 8,000 inhabitants.

A stroll around old Khajurajo is the best way of soaking up an authentic Hindu atmosphere. The house doorways stand open, permitting glimpses of everyday life inside. Busy streets lead to the heart of the village and its central feature, the well. The entire village congregates in this small square where they come to cool off, wash or fetch water.

Panna National Park

The park lies about 50 km (30 miles) from Khajuraho. Its dry vegetation, groves and wooded stretches shelter an abundance of wildlife. Nearby there are diamond mines where you can get an idea of the methods of extraction. Along the road to Panna, you'll see the magnificent **Raneh Falls**, tumbling through luxuriant foliage.

Millions of Hindus come each year to purify themselves in the sacred waters of the goddess Ganga.

Pankaj Shah

Varanasi

Varanasi, formerly known as Benares, is the holy city of the Hindu religion and its religious and cultural centre. A much frequented place of pilgrimage, it's the city where all Hindus dream of dying, because from here the soul passes more quickly to nirvana.

It is also one of the most ancient cities in the world. But its temples have so often been sacked by invaders and its walls so often destroyed by the angry floods of the Ganges that it is difficult to imagine how once it must have looked. The "eternal city" nevertheless lives up to its reputation: in its labyrinthine streets, and by the immense banks and staircases of the sacred river, the atmosphere is permeated with mysticism, and the past is so tangible that Varanasi seems to rise out of the mists of time.

At the heart of an overpopulated rural region, the old town spreads along the western bank of the Ganges. In the interior, the streets lined with tall houses seethe with 1.2 million people. They throng the picturesque markets and rattle through the streets in rickshaws; the air swirls with suffocating dust and intoxicating smells, and cows wander everywhere. There is no comparison with the wide shady avenues of the Cantonment, the modern district of airline offices, large hotels and fashionable restaurants.

You don't visit Varanasi: you see it and breathe it. Most of the temples, such as the Durga and the Bharat Mata, are only of moderate interest, and the finest monuments are closed to the public. That leaves the streets, the *ghats* and the markets.

The Banks of the Ganges

The sacred river, where millions of Hindus come each year to purify themselves in the waters, is one of the world's dirtiest waterways. The level of pollution in the water at Varanasi is about ten times higher than it should be, a situation partly due to chemical fertilizers and the industries of urban centres, not to mention the thousands of pilgrims who cremate their dead on the riverbank. It isn't at all unusual to see the bloated cadavers of animals or the partially incinerated remains of human bodies floating by, and it takes some time to get used to it. Nevertheless, Hindu ascetics maintain that whoever believes in the purity of the river can bathe and drink its holy water without the slightest risk of infection. In fact, every day thousands of Indians come here to perform their *puja* (prayers and offerings) and their ablutions, providing the most fascinating spectacle the city has to offer.

Five ghats on the pilgrim route. At the southern extremity of the old city, **Asai Ghat** is the first of five special stairways assigned as baths. In order to accomplish the great sacrament of purification, they must be visited in a pre-scribed sequence on the same day. After Asai, the pilgrim route proceeds to **Dasaswamedh, Barnasangam, Panchganga** and, lastly, **Manikarnika Ghat.**

Still Thinking

The Ghats

These huge flights of stairs lining the river bank from one end of town to the other are the principal attraction of Varanasi. Because their foundations are below water level, palaces and conical temples tilt ominously. Every monsoon causes more damage. Some of the *ghats*, such as Tulsidas, have collapsed and others have had to be rebuilt.

Many a maharajah wishing to end his days in the holy city built a palace by the river. As a conse-quence, most of the *ghats* belong to them. Between Raj Ghat (to the north) and Nagwa Ghat (to the south) there are some 35 stair-cases of varying width. Notable among them are the **Dasaswamedh**, central and very busy, and the **Manikarnika**, where cremations take place. This ancestral custom is widespread throughout India and is derived from ancient sacred writings which state that fire helps the soul to reach para-dise. Not only is Varanasi the holy city of the Hindus, but it is also the city of death. Hindus from all over India come here to die or to cremate their dead when their financial circumstances per-mit. It is quite common to see funeral processions in the streets. The body, wrapped in red, white or yellow cloth according to the sex and caste of the deceased, is carried on foot to Manikarnika or

Harishchandra Ghat. Only the men accompany the corpse to the funeral pyre.

At night, the sight of burning bodies is amazing. The ashes are borne away by the Ganges. Unfortunately, wood is becoming increasingly expensive and many families can't afford to buy enough to consume the whole body—the reason why half-burnt corpses are regularly thrown into the river. In Varanasi, one man, an Untouchable, has the monopoly of wood sales.

Sacred Steps

The thousands of steps leading down to the river, where so many Hindu legends have flourished, are rich in holy places. Above Manikarnika Ghat, a pool of the same name is filled, so it is said, with the perspiration of Shiva. The god is traditionally held to have dug the well in order to recover the earring which the goddess Parvati dropped in this very place.

At **Charan Paduka**, between the well and the *ghat*, a slab bears the footprints of Vishnu. The footsteps of another celebrated saint are to be seen on the **Dattatreya Ghat** (next to Scindhia Ghat). Further along, near **Trilochan Ghat**, two towers rising from the Ganges mark the point where the water is particularly sacred.

At dawn the light over the *ghats* is at its most spectacular. From the river, the sight of the *sadhu* praying or bathing is unforgettable. The holy city inevitably attracts crowds of these ascetics, who have sacrificed everything for their gods and devote themselves to meditation, living entirely by charity. For Indians, rejection of the world and begging are two of the paths that lead to nirvana, the state of perfect peace of mind and freedom from suffering.

The legend of the Ganges. The Ganges is the sacred river of India. For Hindus, it symbolizes the beneficent and impetuous goddess Ganga, who came to earth to purify the ashes of the 60,000 sons of King Sagara. These were incinerated by the flash of anger of the sage Kapila when they tried to steal the divine horse with which he was entrusted. The goddess, however, was not at all keen on the idea of leaving her native Himalayas. She accepted the challenge, but immediately announced that her torrential waters would flood the plains of India. However, Shiva caught the torrent in his hair before letting it run slowly to earth. Images of the god catching the Ganges in his hair are widespread throughout the country.

A *sadhu* finds some privacy to continue his route towards nirvana.

Although every *sadhu* hopes to reach nirvana, the way of redemption is not the same for all. The followers of Shiva and Vishnu illustrate the two principal existing lines of thought. The first can be recognized by three horizontal lines painted on their foreheads, while those devoted to Vishnu have a yellow U daubed between the eyebrows, sometimes with the addition of a red line. In imitation of the gods they worship, they wind their long hair, which is never cut, into a topknot. If they wear clothes, the colour of their garments reflects the degree of renunciation they have attained, or the specific way of life they have chosen. However, some *sadhu* live naked and cover their skin with ashes, which gives them a ghostly appearance. A symbol of death, ashes are considered to be impure, and the holy men who do this are demonstrating their denial of society and their submission to Shiva, the god of destruction and eternal renewal.

Chowk

The old district of Varanasi the Chowk is an intricate labyrinth of shopping lanes, stalls and cheap restaurants only a few steps away from the *ghats*. The only way to explore this area is on foot, so narrow is the space between the houses.

Golden Temple

Kashi Vishwanath, the Golden Temple dedicated to Shiva, stands at the heart of the commercial area of the Chowk, halfway between Panchganga Ghat and Gai Ghat. This superb shrine topped with a golden dome was rebuilt opposite its original site after the Moghul emperor Aurangzeb had it destroyed in order to make way for a mosque. For the construction of the new temple in 1776, 750 kg (1,650 lb) of gold were required. The building is hidden behind a high wall and almost invisible from the street, and entry is forbidden to non-Hindus. The only way to see it is to climb onto the roof of an adjacent house.

Beside the temple, the **Gyan Kupor**, or Well of Knowledge, is one of the most venerated holy places in the country. It is where Shiva's famous lingam was hidden to keep it safe from the invading Muslims.

Mosques of Aurangzeb

The **Gyanvapi Mosque** is as inaccessible as the Golden Temple opposite. Built by the Moghul emperor on the ruins of the great temple to Shiva, some traces of which remain, it is a perpetual source of conflict between the Hindu and Muslim communities. Consequently, it is guarded by hundreds of armed soldiers and protected by miles of barbed wire. You can see only the minarets, more than 70 m (230 ft) high.

From the 11th century onwards, Varanasi was pillaged over and over again by Muslim invaders. Aurangzeb, completing the destruction, reduced almost all the temples to ruins. On the bank of the Ganges, just above Panchganga Ghat, **Alamgir Mosque** was built on the site of an ancient temple dedicated to Vishnu. It combines an unusual mixture of Hindu and Muslim architecture.

Hindu Temples

The 18th-century **Temple of Durga**, or Monkey Temple, is the most famous of the town's Hindu shrines but is closed to the public, apart from the courtyard where you can admire its red ochre colour and typical North Indian Nagara style. The multi-tiered *shikhara*, or spire, symbolizes the elements and represents Brahma.

The white marble **Tulsi Manas Temple**, next door, was built in 1964 and commemorates the poet Tulsi Das. It is open for visits.

Also open to the public, **Bharat Mata Temple** on Vidyapath Road in the northwest of town was inaugurated by Ghandi and dedicated to Mother India. Inside is a giant relief map of India carved in marble.

Sarnath

Buddha is said to have preached his first sermon 2,500 years ago at Sarnath, only 10 km (6 miles) north of Varanasi. On this sacred site, Emperor Ashoka, a convert to Buddhism and non-violence after he had murdered several members of his own family and hundreds of thousands on the battlefield, established a religious centre that remained very active until it was destroyed by the Muslims. Of the temples and monasteries of Ashoka's time, only ruins remain.

Shiva's *lingam*. Varanasi is devoted to Shiva, represented as being gaunt, with dishevelled hair and coated with ashes. His rigorous discipline raises him above the other divinities. He is the god of procreative energies and a yoga master capable of transmuting them into a spiritual force. Because of this power, the *lingam*, or phallus, is the principal symbol of Shiva worship and the sign of the absolute. It is a column with no beginning or end, representing the cosmic pillar, an axis that holds up the universe. The *lingam* seen in most of Shiva's temples or on the ghats of Varanasi is a miniature version of this supreme pillar. All over India, the *lingam* is depicted inside a *yoni* (the female symbol).

The site itself is of limited interest, but the archaeological collection in the museum is worth a visit. One of the prize exhibits is the capital of the famous pillar of Ashoka. Made of polished sandstone, the column was erected around 250 BC and stood more than 17 m (56 ft) high. It is now in several pieces, preserved in the original site. The capital has been adapted as the official emblem of modern India; it takes the form of four lions back to back, mounted on a cylindrical abacus featuring an elephant, a horse, a bull and a lion alternating with 24-spoked Dharma wheels over a bell-shaped lotus.

Ramnagar
Some 20 km (12 miles) southeast of Varanasi, the fort of Ramnagar is still the home of the town's former maharajah. Part of his palace has been converted into a museum, overflowing with luxurious and intriguing objects acquired by generations of maharajahs. Among them you'll see an astrological clock, antique weapons, palanquins of brocade and silver and elephant caparisons. The fort is also used as a film location.

istockphoto.com/Skiphunt

www.viajar24h.com

Os Rúpias

Silk saris drying in the sun. | **The Ganges may be polluted, but it is still revered as a sacred river.** | **Buddha looks in all four directions at Sarnath.**

Your cup of Darjeeling starts right here at the foot of the Himalayas.

Thomas Petrochilo

West Bengal

When they needed respite from the heat of Calcutta (now Kolkata), the British went up into the hills and the cool greenery of the tea plantations of Darjeeling, close to the border with Tibet, beneath the snowy white peaks of the Himalayas. This corner of India is also home to the Sundarbans, the tiger's favourite jungle haunt, located a half-day's journey southeast of Kolkata by car and boat.

Kolkata

A pungent mixture of Imperial splendour with equal parts of Bengali intelligence, squalor and overcrowding, Kolkata is not for the faint-hearted. India's intellectual and cultural capital, it was the home of philosophers Ramakrishna and Vivekananda, and India's first Nobel Prize winner Rabindranath Tagore. It also has the Indian Museum—one of the country's best.

Howrah

Howrah Station, packed with an unbelievable number of people, makes a stupendous and eye-opening introduction to the city. Built in 1943, the steel suspension Howrah Bridge sweeps over the river to the city centre. Its lower deck, where the road passes, is practically a solid traffic jam. The bathing ghats are located beneath the bridge at the station end, where men bathe and women do the laundry, while at the Calcutta end is the colourful **Mullik Ghat Flower Market**.

Botanical Gardens

For respite from the teeming crowds on the station side of the Hooghly River, head for the Botanical Gardens stretching along the bank further south. The first tea cuttings were brought here from China to found the plantations of Darjeeling and Assam. A 200-year-old banyan tree, covering a ground area of 400 m (437 yd) in circumference, is claimed to be the largest in the world.

Memories of the Raj

Scattered around the streets of central Calcutta are architectural relics of the Raj in varying states of decay, with crumbling plasterwork and flaking stucco, trees taking root in the brickwork and grandiose archways opening onto uninviting courtyards. The long, landscaped **Maidan** park around Fort William is a gathering place for all and sundry; it is often compared with Hyde Park because of its soap-box orators, but any resemblance ends there.

An air of dignity surrounds the palatial Anglo-Renaissance **Victoria Memorial**, built in 1921 of white marble (from the same quarries used for the Taj Mahal). It was commissioned by Viceroy Lord Curzon during the days of the Raj, and paid for by "voluntary" contributions from the maharajahas and people of India. The architect was Sir William Emerson. Inside, displays of portraits, statues, busts and other memorabilia tell the tale of the British Empire at its peak.

The busiest shopping street is **Jawaharlal Nehru Road**, along the east side of the Maidan at the limits of the old European neighbourhood.

The infamous Black Hole of Calcutta has long since disappeared, but you can see a plaque marking its site in an arch at the northeast corner of the splendid domed **General Post Office** (built 1864–68) on the west side of Dalhousie Square (also called BBD Bagh). At the water's edge, people sit beneath the trees or fish. Nearby is the **Writers' Building**, once the headquarters of the East India Company and the centre of Imperial bureaucracy, and now used by the Government of West Bengal.

Near the magnificent Governor's Residence (Raj Bhavan), with Imperial lions on its two arches, **St John's Church** (1787) stands in a large, grassy churchyard. It was the city's first cathedral, built on the model of London's St Martin in the Fields. The octagonal monument in the churchyard is the tomb (1695) of Job Charnock, the English merchant who founded the city. In the church's south aisle, a painting of *The Last Supper* uses members of the East India Company as models for the saints. The artist, John Zoffany, depicted his enemy Mr Paull as Judas.

Marble Palace

In the north of town near the Mahatma Gandhi Road metro station, in Muktaram Babu Street, the Marble Palace is a huge Palladian villa transformed into a museum. Its eclectic exhibits include ancient Roman and Chinese sculpture, Sèvres porcelain, Venetian glass and paintings by Rubens and Sir Joshua Reynolds.

Indian Museum

At the crossing of Nehru Road and Sudder Street, the Indian Museum should not be missed. It displays treasures from the ancient Maurya and Gupta eras, with splendid Buddhist carvings in the Bharbut Gallery, and, in the Gandhara Room, the earliest sculptures representing Buddha in a human form, from the 1st century.

Darjeeling

Now part of West Bengal, Darjeeling was situated in the then independent kingdom of Sikkim until 1835, when the rajah was pressured into ceding it to the British. The official language remains Nepali, and most of the people are of Nepalese or Tibetan origin. A scenic way up to the town is by the miniature **Darjeeling Himalayan Railway**, which begins at Siliguri. Rather than digging tunnels, the railway builders of 1881 took the tracks round the mountains, so you still get breathtaking views of the valleys and terraced tea gardens, rippling over the slopes like green velvet corduroy.

Os Rúpias

The mountains bring welcome cool air to Darjeeling.

The streets of Darjeeling are steep, and its buildings, typical of many hill stations, are of wood with tin roofs and gables trimmed with fretwork. There is a **monument to Tensing**, the Sherpa who, along with Sir Edmund Hillary, was the first man to climb Mount Everest.

Tiger Hill
A popular outing is a pre-dawn drive to Tiger Hill, where, from an observation platform you can see **Mount Kanchenjunga** and, on specially clear days, a glimpse of the distant jagged peak of Everest. From here it's possible to walk to the railway station at **Ghoom**. The **Yellow Hat monastery** below the station is open to visitors; you can listen to the Buddhist monks reading from scriptures written on scrolls that are stacked in pigeonholes around the walls.

Kalimpong
You can also travel to Kalimpong via the Teesta River Bridge. This hill station is a fairly quiet bazaar town of 41,000, at an altitude of 1,250 m (4,100 ft) and was a centre for Scottish missionaries in the late 19th century. You can visit three monasteries, a silk-worm-breeding centre and orchid nurseries, or study the Tibetan and Himalayan language and culture in a private library. Market days are Wednesday and Saturday.

Gangtok
The journey to the Sikkim capital, Gangtok (at 1,768 m, 5,800 ft), is superb, through deep valleys etched with terraces of rice fields and forested hills. Here and there, the landscape is dotted with white stupas or *gortens*. Gangtok has an **Insitute of Tibetology**, with a large collection of books and rare manuscripts on the subject of Mahayana Buddhism, and fine

silk embroidered cloth paintings (*thankas*). Surrounding the institute is the **Orchid Sanctuary**.

Monasteries

In the distance you can see the **Rumtek monastery**, 24 km (15 miles) away by road. It is the seat of the Gyalwa Karmapa, the leader of the Kagyupa sect of Buddhism, founded in the 11th century. The mural paintings here are exquisite. Visitors are welcome, and you may get to taste Tibetan salted tea with yak butter blended into it.

Two other 18th-century monasteries worth visiting are **Tashiding**, with its brightly painted frescoes, and **Pemayangtse**, 150 km (92 miles) west of Gangtok. Surrounded by snow-capped mountains, Pemayangtse is one of the state's most important monasteries. It belongs to the Tantric Nyingmapa sect, established in the 8th century. Outside, coloured prayer flags flutter in the breeze and the atmosphere is incredibly pure and holy. On three storeys, the building is full of wall paintings and sculpture, among which you can admire a seven-tiered model of paradise and hell.

Sundarbans National Park

At the estuary of the Ganges-Brahmaputra delta on the Bay of Bengal, the park extends east to India's frontier with Bangladesh.

India's part of Sundarbans, a UNESCO World Heritage site since 1997, covers some 4,000 of the park's total area of 10,000 sq km.

The Royal Bengal tigers, as these man-eaters are known here, share with wild boar, spotted chital deer and rhesus monkeys a habitat of dense mangrove forest on a cluster of islands scattered across the delta. The tigers are great swimmers, covering large distances in search of their supper. Their numbers have dwindled here to fewer than 200, with perhaps the same number again on the Bangladeshi side.

From the tourist lodge at **Sajnekhali**, most safaris into the Sundarbans Tiger Reserve take the form of boat cruises along the great rivers' myriad tributaries. On the way, you may also spot the formidable estuarine crocodiles, along with Olive Ridley sea turtles, dolphins and sharks. In the **Sajnekhali Bird Sanctuary**, look out for long-beaked whimbrel, black-tailed godwit, little stint, eastern knot, golden plover, whistling teal and white bellied sea eagle. The park's human residents eke out a living from fishing, collecting honey and cutting timber. For protection against the wild beasts, they—and you—can look to Ma Bonobi, the forest's goddess, Shiber Kumir, Shiva's crocodile-god, and Dakshinaroy, divine ancestor of all tigers.

THE BACKDROP

Chaupar

This game derives from the same origins as chess, like *pachisi* and *chaturanga*. The name, from the Sanskrit *catus-pada*, means "four-legged". Chaupar (or *caupur*) is played on a cross-shaped board or two pieces of cloth and is similar to the English game of ludo. The players throw dice to determine the number of moves the pieces can make, travelling all round the board to finish in the middle. It is still played in some villages. Antique sets—boards of embroidered cloth and ivory pieces—are sold at exorbitant prices in antique shops. More recent versions in wood can be found at bric-a-brac stalls.

Cinema

In India the silver screen is the opium of the masses. The country has thousands of cinemas and video halls, and produces more films than anywhere else in the world: an average of 850 each year. Two cities share the spoils: Chennai (Madras) and Mumbai (Bombay), whose gigantic film studios are nicknamed "Bollywood". Indian films, generally cheap melodramas, are aimed at the poorest sections of the population, the middle classes preferring more commercial American films.

The so-called masala movies provide the cocktail most likely to offer the cinema-goers escapism from their daily problems: one half love scenes, a generous splash of singing and dancing and a sprinkling of violence. They may last two and a half hours and include 18 songs.

Meena Kadri

Clothing

The long white cotton tunic with matching trousers is rare nowadays. While the young people like to dress in Western style, most men still keep to the simple *dhoti*, a length of fabric worn around the hips and pulled up between the legs, with a loose, light-coloured shirt on top. You'll see a lot of women in T-shirts and skirts or jeans, but most remain faithful to the sari, about a metre wide and 5 to 9 m long, draped around the body with the *pallav*, (the elaborately decorated end), thrown gracefully over the left shoulder, or sometimes lifted over the head. It seems to stay in place miraculously, without any pins or buttons to hold it down. Beneath it, women wear a *choli*, a short blouse. At one time, the way the sari was draped depended on the region and ethnic background. The colour used to be significant, too: white for mourning, red for a wedding, but these customs are gradually disappearing.

Music

Cinema, television and radio pour out endless floods of nondescript songs mingling traditional folk songs and Western pop music. Authentic Indian music, rarely broadcast by the media, is nevertheless alive and well. Transmitted from father to son for at least two millennia, it can be heard at popular gatherings, village festivals and religious gatherings. A marriage of oral tradition and improvisation, it leaves the performer free to add personal touches.

In the south, karnatic music— purely Hindu—has not evolved since its origins. In the north, Muslim influence has resulted in the more spiritual Hindustani Vedic music. It has two basic elements: *tala*, the rhythm, characterized by a certain number of beats, and *raga*, the melody, in addition to a background drone. There is no harmony, in the Western sense, and each musician chooses his own *tala* and *raga*.

The best-known instruments are the sitar and the tabla. The *raga* is played on the sitar, usually made of teak wood and with 20 strings. The tabla is a

Toby Forage

drum of camelskin and beats out the rhythm, while the *baga*, a kind of harmonium, provides the drone. The *sarangui* is a complex stringed instrument played with a bow. Some instruments have a symbolic significance. The *shehnai* (oboe) is played on festive occasions and the *bankia* or the *dhonsa* (both types of trumpet) herald the arrival of an important person — or the imminence of war.

Sport

You have only to see the number of TV sets placed in shop windows or in restaurants during international matches to confirm your suspicions that cricket, introduced by the British in the 19th century, is still India's favourite sport, and in the villages you'll often see children enthusiastically batting in front of makeshift wickets, even with tennis balls.

This enthusiasm reaches all layers of society, to the point where one TV channel is devoted exclusively to the game. The passions aroused by certain matches — India versus Pakistan, for example — go well beyond sporting limits. Nevertheless, cricket is the traditionally gentlemanly game, synonymous with fair play.

Field hockey has provided India with some of its finest sporting successes. Initiated by British officers at the end of the 19th century, Indians now play this game to perfection: they carried off all the Olympic competitions from 1928 to 1956, scoring 32 goals while losing only three. But Pakistan put an end to their supremacy in 1960 at Melbourne.

Football, developing fast, has not yet reached the level of popularity of cricket. India can not yet enter its team in international competitions.

John Haslam

Rajasthan artist, painting in the ancient miniature style.

Renata Holzbachová

SHOPPING

The richness and diversity of crafts in northern India reflect its history and various cultures. The quality of the work, from woven silks through jewellery to inlaid marble, bear witness to techniques passed down from generation to generation.

Where

A visit to the official state shops of the State Emporia Complex on Baba Kharag Singh Avenue (near Connaught Place) or to the Central Cottage Industries on Janpath in Delhi will provide a good overview of the full range of crafts available in this part of India. The prices are fixed and will give you an idea of the cost of items before you embark on a shopping expedition in the bazaars, where you must be prepared to bargain hard. Another possibility is to visit the shopping galleries in the large hotels or in the fashionable parts of town. Prices there are fixed—and high.

Scams and swindles

Varanasi, Jaipur and Agra are crawling with commission merchants and swindlers. Many of the shops claim to be official state shops, but they are not, and touts will surround tourists on the pretext of offering advice. Rickshaw and taxi drivers and official guides are all paid commission for bringing a client into a shop. This can be as much as 40 per cent of the cost of the goods, and you will be footing the bill. The first price asked by a shopkeeper is usually three or four times the real value of the article. If you pay with a credit card, do not let it out of your sight. Make sure the slip is filled out in front of you, not in a back room where they may be imprinting extra slips and forging your signature.

Jewellery

Jaipur is famous for precious and semi-precious stones. You can bargain for the former at Haldion ka Rasta and the latter at Gopalji ka Rasta, near Johari Bazaar. This is where the traditional jewellery, *meenakari*, is produced—combining gold, gemstones and floral designs in enamel. They also make items in classical Indian or European styles. But be careful:

there are many counterfeits and cheap items sold for ten times their value, even in well-established jewelleries. It is better to avoid M.I. Road.

Nobody wears jewellery more imaginatively than the Indians, and if you want to follow suit, take a look at how the gorgeous princesses do it in a classical Bollywood musical—not just the rings on their toes as well as their fingers but, besides the multicoloured necklaces and brooches, a profusion of bangles on their ankles as well as wrists. Many bazaar stalls sell nothing but bangles—silver, gold, copper, glass, lacquered wood and, cheapest of all, gorgeous varnished papier-mâché pieces from Kashmir.

Marble

The walls of the Taj Mahal are decorated with semi-precious stones, cut, carved and inlaid in white marble. In Nai ki Mandi, the old Muslim quarter of Agra, or in the state companies within the Cantonment, all kinds of objects are manufactured in the same way: tables, ashtrays, chessboards, etc. The time required to produce a piece is considerable—three months for the lid of a small box, six months for a tray.

Carpets

In Jaipur, the manufacture of wool or silk carpets is a tradition which goes back to the 18th century. Traditionally, the colours are obtained from saffron, sugar cane, indigo and iron oxide. The quality and price are fixed by the number of knots: 288 knots per square inch for a cheap wool carpet from Rajasthan, 580 for a Kashmir carpet and up to 1,800 or 2,000 for a silk carpet. Depending on the quality, a carpet can cost anything from 5,000 to 10,000 rupees.

Cotton dhurries woven with geometrical designs in bright colours made from vegetable dyes are a speciality of Agra. You'll find them in the main street of the old Muslim quarter. They cost only a few dozen rupees.

Textiles

India is especially strong in textiles. Silk fabrics are best bought in Varanasi, where they are woven by hand and printed in natural colours using a technique exclusive to the workshops of Madanpura Road. Production is targeted at the manufacture of the sari. The boutiques of Chowk offer an unrivalled choice. Silk is sold by weight, expressed in grams per metre.

The Jaipur region enjoys another proud tradition—block-printed tablecloths, napkins, bedspreads and saris. Also in Jaipur, at the Johari Bazaar, cottons and *kadhi* (hand-woven fabrics) in bright colours are sold by the yard.

These hand-printed or embroidered cottons constitute northern India's best bargain for the budget-conscious shopper. Look out for napkins, table-cloths, bed-linen, especially the spectacular bedspreads and matching pillow-cases. A good idea to buy at the outset of your trip would be a long, airy thin cotton scarf to make life much more comfortable in the prickly Indian heat. By the same token, you might want to invest right away in light-weight cotton shirts and even a baggy pair of trousers, made to measure — Indian tailors are cheap and will make them up for you in just a few hours.

And more...

Copper items and bronze statuettes are found everywhere, as are miniature paintings copied on antique paper. You'll also see attractive engraved and lacquered brassware and blue pottery in Jaipur. Antique shops are overflowing with fine pieces. Stock up on spices in the markets: saffron is good value and the pepper fragrant.

Printed bags to carry your souvenirs home. | **Mirrored patchwork to keep away the evil spirits.** | **Powder to paint a tika on your forehead.** | **Glass bangles.**

Nomad Tales

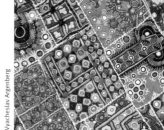
Vyacheslav Argenberg

Felipe Skroski

bengal*foam

Thali is often served on a banana leaf and eaten with the fingers.

Salvatore Barbera

DINING OUT

Northern India, unlike the South, is not exclusively vegetarian and its specialities are less highly spiced, although curries are the basis of the daily diet. Indian cookery combines all the exotic flavours of a country rich in spices—cardamom, cloves, ginger, pepper. It is perfectly acceptable to eat with your fingers.

Curries

These are India's staple dish. Curry is not a plant nor even the yellow powder on supermarket shelves, but a subtle blend of spices (masala), which includes cumin, coriander and fenugreek, to which are added garlic, a few cloves, a generous pinch of nutmeg, anise, bay leaves and pepper. The slightly bitter turmeric gives a rich yellow colour to Indian curries. It's sometimes called "poor man's saffron", because it has the same golden colour, if not the same flavour, as saffron and is much less costly. Paprika is often used instead of turmeric and gives a dark red colour. Each family has its own recipe for this sauce, which accompanies most vegetables and diced or minced meats. Curry comes with rice, vegetables, yoghurt (raita), chutneys (mango, lime, aubergine, etc.), pickles and bread (puri, chapati, roti).

Mughlai Meat

Northern India's classical cuisine is known as Mughlai, from the Moghols who brought together Persian, Afghan and Rajput culinary traditions. Excluding the Hindus' taboo on beef and the Muslim taboo on pork, the dominant meat dishes are of lamb or mutton, and chicken tandoori-style. The most common mutton curry is rogan josh, cooked in a yoghurt sauce spiced with ginger, chilli, coriander and an aromatic garam masala blend of cloves, cinnamon and cardamom.

The northern Indian version of kebab barbecues balls of lamb minced with spices, almonds and pistachios. Fit for a maharajah and often the centrepiece of a wedding banquet inherited from Kashmir, goshtaba is the tenderest piece of lamb taken from the breast with all its sinews removed and minced in a spicy dumpling stewed in yoghurt.

A favourite of Indian restaurants worldwide, *biryani* is also a Mughlai speciality in which the meat—lamb or chicken—is cooked in a spicy sauce and then steamed with saffron rice and *ghee* (clarified butter). It can be decoratively served with mint, almonds and even an airy-thin edible piece of silver foil to add a touch of opulence. You can also find vegetarian *biryani*, and *pulao* rice dishes.

Dhal

This is northern India's favourite dish. Nourishing and cheap, it consists of a rather sloppy hot and spicy lentil curry accompanied by plain rice and *chapati*. In restaurants, you can generally eat as much *dhal* as you like. Many Indians eat it every day.

Thali

Although originally a traditional dish of the south, the *thali* is now found all over India. It was inspired by the ancient principles of traditional medicine, and is supposed to supply all the necessary proteins, vitamins and daily dose of garlic and ginger. It comprises various vegetable curries, *dhal* and spices with rice and *chapati*. In the best restaurants, a sweet item is included. The whole lot is served on a honeycombed metal or plastic dish, or more simply on a banana leaf.

Tandoori cooking

Highly flavoured *tandoori*-style cooking is very popular. This is again a speciality of the north. The *tandoor* is a clay oven with very hot embers inside. Air circulates through side openings and keeps the fire burning brightly. The high temperature means that chicken, skewers of meat and various cuts, previously marinated in a mixture of flavourings and yoghurt, can be cooked rapidly. Baked in the same oven, *naan* is a flat bread flavoured with garlic, onions or butter.

Paan

Paan is the Indian equivalent of chewing gum, primarily taken after a meal as an aid to digestion. Consisting of a betel leaf wrapped around a mixture of lime ash, areca nut, *catachu* powder, various spices and condiments such as coconut, cardamom, cashew, dried rose petals and tobacco, even opium, it is mildly intoxicating and addictive, and Indians can chew it all day long. Recipes vary from region to region and according to the paan-wallah who mixes and sells it. Chewing *paan* turns your mouth red and your teeth black. After they've extracted the last drop of juice from their mouthful, people spit out the leftovers—an unappealing habit that leaves eloquent red blotches all over the streets.

Desserts

Indians notoriously have a sweet tooth, and there are plenty of syrupy desserts and various intriguing and colourful goodies on street stalls and in shops. Most sweets, such as *gulab jamun* and *barfi*, are based on boiled, thickened milk with different flavourings. Coconut, rose water, pistachio and almond are frequently used. Rice and chick-pea flour form the basis for other desserts; while *gajar ka halwa* is made from grated carrots boiled until translucent in milk and sugar. Melons, green coconuts and mangoes are the most delicious fruits.

Nitin Badhwar

Drinks

Most Indians never drink alcohol. Their favourite refresher is a glass of *chai*, hot, sweet, spicy, milky tea. Otherwise, *lassi* is a delicious liquid yoghurt, served sweetened or salted, and occasionally in clay pots which are thrown away after use.

Renata Holzbachová

Soft drinks tend to be sickly, but there are plenty of good fruit juices sold in cartons. Local beer is not bad at all, though not so easy to find, and India even produces wine. Mineral water is sold in plastic bottles.

Chole kulche—spicy chickpeas with bread. | An elegant *thali*. | Make sure you get it right.

Nicholas Kenrick

Don't worry if your cellphone doesn't work; there are plenty of other solutions.

THE HARD FACTS

To help with your travel plans, here are some useful facts about Northern India.

Airports
Indira Gandhi International airport (DEL) is 22 km (15 miles) south of Delhi. It is linked to the centre by the rapid and modern metro, with its terminus at the central station. Several airlines compete to serve most big cities. Only a few are neglected, like Agra and Jaisalmer. Flights are often booked up, so reserve seats early during holidays.

Climate
The best season for travelling in the North is from October to March. The heat is stifling in spring, 35–40°C (95–104°F), and summer is the monsoon season. In autumn and winter the temperature is about 25–30°C (77–86°F) during the day and can fall to 8°C (46°F) at night. Rainfall is rare at this time of the year.

Clothing
Choose clothing appropriate to a hot climate. However, don't forget a sweater and a jacket, because the evenings can be cool and the restaurants air-conditioned. Almost all hotels offer a rapid laundry service. That being said, you'll find very good value light-weight clothing of Indian or European style almost everywhere. There are also shops specializing in made-to-measure tailoring. To visit mosques and other Muslim monuments, you should dress modestly.

Currency
The Indian *rupee* (Rs) is divided into 100 *paise*. Coins are issued with values of 25 and 50 paise and 1 to 10 rupees; banknotes in circulation range from 1 to 100 Rs. It is impossible to obtain rupees in the West, but no matter what time you arrive in India there'll be an exchange office open at the airport. The best solution is to take US dollars in cash or travellers cheques, which are easy to change. The Euro is accepted in most places, but at an unfavourable rate of exchange. It's advisable to refuse torn notes, as no one will accept them apart from the National Bank.

Credit cards are accepted in the big hotels and restaurants and in most fixed-price shops.

Electricity
The voltage is usually 220 AC. 50 Hz. Plugs have two or three round pins.

Entry Formalities
You need a valid passport and a visa to enter India. Tourist visas are valid for up to six months. They are obtainable from the Indian Embassy in your home country and can take some time, so apply well in advance. You have to present a passport valid for at least six months beyond your departure date and pay a fee which varies from year to year.

Passengers over 17 may import into India 200 cigarettes or 50 cigars or 250 g tobacco; 2 litres wine or spirits.

Essentials
Basic toiletries (soap, razors, toothbrushes, tampons) are available in Indian and some Western brands. It is always useful to have a first-aid kit with you (with anti-diarrhoea tablets, for example), and any special medication you will need. Take a torch—electricity cuts are frequent—and anti-mosquito cream.

Health
Although no vaccinations are obligatory, doctors highly recommend vaccination against hepatitis A and typhoid fever, and booster shots for tetanus and poliomyelitis. Depending on the length and type of your stay, it may also be wise to be vaccinated against hepatitis B and Japanese encephalitis. As for malaria, in view of the risk, it is best to follow a preventive treatment and to take reserve supplies with you.

To stay in good health, be careful about what you drink and eat. Above all, never drink water straight from the tap. To make it safe, use purification tablets or boil the water for at least 20 minutes. If you buy bottled mineral water, make sure the top is hermetically sealed; often, labelled bottles are refilled with tap water. Stay clear, too, of ice cubes and ice-cream, and beware of fruit juices diluted with water. Milk is often unpasteurized.

Eat only well-cooked food, and fruit you have peeled yourself.

Holidays and Festivals
These are numerous and usually movable, following the Indian lunar calendar, so it is advisable to enquire about holidays in advance of your trip.

The best-known is Diwali, the Hindu festival of light, celebrated in October and November. The spring festival, Holi, in February or March is the occasion for people to sprinkle everyone they meet with coloured powder. Republic Day is fixed on January 26 and commemorates the founding of the Republic in 1950. It is marked by a splendid parade along Delhi's Rajpath with elephants and camels. In Rajasthan, the spring Gangaur Festival is held in honour of Gauri (Parvati), the consort of Shiva, and is auspicious for finding a husband or ensuring a long and happy married life. The similar Teej takes place in summer, it is goddess Parvati's day.

India is a multicultural country and also celebrates Ramadan, Christmas and many other religious or regional festivals.

Languages

Since Independence, the official language of India is Hindi, while English is the subsidiary official language used for administration and in business and the tourist industry. All educated Indians speak fluent English and many people have at least a basic grasp. The Constitution recognizes 22 regional languages, including Assamese, Bengali, Gujerati and Urdu, and there are 400 dialects without official status.

Media

Most national papers are published in Hindi. There are excellent dailies in English, such as the *Times of India* or the *The Hindu*, *The Economic Times* and *The Statesman*. Weeklies include *Frontline* and *India Today*.

Opening Hours

They vary according to place and branch. Banks, post offices, shops and embassies open between 8.30 and 10 a.m. and close between 6 and 7 p.m. in Delhi, working 1 or 2 hours less in the rest of the country. The bank's exchange desk closes in the early afternoon, but service companies and small shops generally keep longer hours. New Delhi's night bazaar opens to 10 p.m. Sunday is the official closing day, except in the Muslim districts.

Post

Stamps are on sale in post offices, certain shops and hotels. The service is extremely erratic, and mail may take several weeks to arrive at its destination.

Telephone

There are many telephone agencies in the towns, identifiable by the letters STD for international calls and ISD for the inland service. To make an international call, dial 00, the country code (1 for US and Canada, 44 for UK) and the local number. The price is indicated on a meter. You can buy local SIM cards for your mobile phone which can be used by prior agreement with your home operator and with proof of accommodation in India. Internet cafés are widespread and rates are often cheaper than in hotels.

Time

All India is within the same time zone, UTC/GMT +5^1/$_2$, so it is 5^1/$_2$ hours ahead of Britain in winter and 4^1/$_2$ hours ahead in summer.

Tipping

Indians, all attuned to the habit of *baksheesh*, demand a tip for the slightest service. The custom bears no relation to gratuities in Europe, being more of a way to ensure decent service rather than expressing thanks. The usual rate is 10–20 Rs for porters and waiters. In the large hotels, it is usual to add 5 or 10 per cent to the bill for the staff. However, you are not expected to tip taxi drivers. The term *baksheesh* is also used by beggars.

Toilets

In the upper or medium categories of hotel, the facilities correspond to Western standards and toilet paper is available for the client. Elsewhere, you will have to contend with holes in the ground. Many Indians find that the use of toilet paper is unhygienic, preferring to use water. If you find this difficult, then you should carry your own paper, on sale everywhere.

Transport

Distances between Delhi, Jaipur and Agra are quite short, but travel is slow. Traffic is dense and chaotic once you approach the cities.

The train is cheap and the ideal method of travel in this region. Express trains are reasonably comfortable, but it's best to choose first class if you want to travel by night. For reliable information on timetables see www.indianrail. gov.in; you can book tickets online but there are some restrictions for visitors. Delhi central station has a special office for non-residents on the first floor, and attributes a limited number of seats on the trains to them.

Intercity coaches are generally comfortable and air-conditioned, but the journeys are long. You can rent a chauffeur-driven car with local companies, at hotels and the regional tourist offices; prices are reasonable. Budget and Hertz operate from Delhi and Jaipur. Be aware that most Indian roads are a nightmare, especially after dark.

The most practical and inexpensive way of getting around the towns is by auto-rickshaw or tuk-tuk, powered by a motorcycle engine, with seats for two or more passengers behind. They are much faster than taxis as they can nip in and out of the traffic, but settle the price beforehand. The cycle rickshaw, with two passenger seats, is dying out.

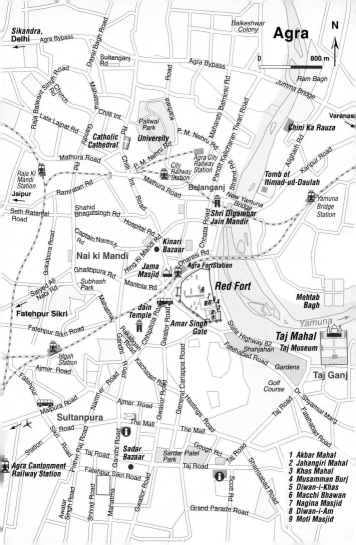

Agra

N

0   800 m

Sikandra, Delhi
Agra Bypass
Sultanganj Rd
Agra Bypass
Balkeshwar Colony
Ram Bagh
Jumma Bridge

Deyal Bagh Road
Raja Balwant Singh Rd
Church Rd
Mahatma Gandhi
Chilli Int.
Paliwal Park
University
P. M. Nehru Rd
Pandit Kalicharan Tiwari Road
Madanshi Balmiki Rd
Chini Ka Rauza

Varanas

Catholic Cathedral
P. M. Nehru Rd
Mathura Road
City Railway Station
Agra City Railway Station
Strand Rd
Aligarh Rd
Kanpur Road
Tomb of Itimad-ud-Daulah

Raja Ki Mandi Station
Jaipur
Ramratan Rd
Mathura Road
Chilli Int.
Belanganj
New Yamuna Bridge
Yamuna Bridge Station

Seth Ratanlal Road
Shahid Bhagatsingh Rd
Hospital Rd
Shri Digambar Jain Mandir
Chhatta Rd

Captain Naresh Rd
Nai ki Mandi
Ghalibpura Rd
King Ki Mandi Rd
Kinari Bazaar
Dharesi Rd
Agra FortStation
Red Fort

Gokulpura Road
Sayyed Ali Nabi Rd
Subhash Park
Jama Masjid
Mantola Rd
Mehtab Bagh

Fatehpur Sikri
Jain Temple
Rakaban Gandhi Rd
Chhipitola Rd
Gwalior Road
Amar Singh Gate
State Highway 62
Shahjahan
Fatehabad Road
Yamuna
Taj Mahal
Taj Museum

Fatehpur Sikri Road
Idgah Station
Ajmer Road
Kachahari Road
Gardens
Golf Course
Taj Ganj

Fatehpur
Malpura Road
Namner Road
Ajmer Road
Gwalior Road
General Cariappa Road
Hastings Road
D. Shyamlal Marg

Station Rd
Sikri Road
Sultanpura
The Mall
The Mall
Gough Rd
Taj Road
Fatehabad Road

Agra Cantonment Railway Station
Prithvi Raj Rd
Taj Rd
Gandhi Road
Sadar Bazaar
Sardar Park
Taj Road
Shamsabad Road

Awatar Singh Road
Shivaji Road
Fatehpur Sikri Road
Mahatma Gandhi Road
Gwalior Road
Grand Parade Road
Scott Rd.

1 Akbar Mahal
2 Jahangiri Mahal
3 Khas Mahal
4 Musamman Burj
5 Diwan-i-Khas
6 Macchi Bhawan
7 Nagina Masjid
8 Diwan-i-Am
9 Moti Masjid

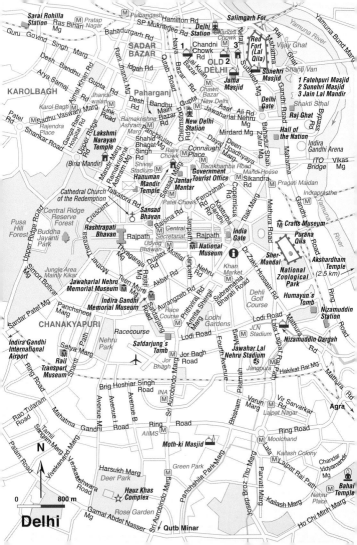

Delhi

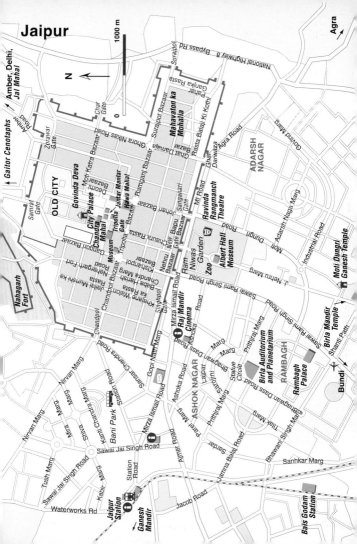

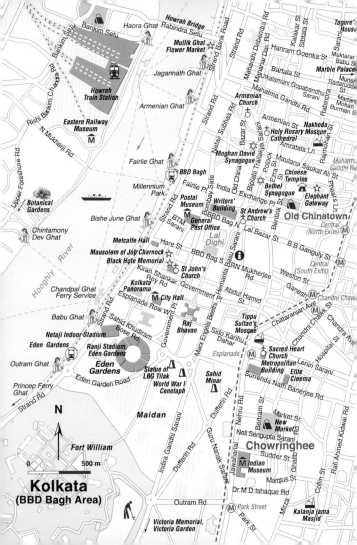

Kolkata
(BBD Bagh Area)

N

0   500 m

Bankim Setu
Haora Ghat
Howrah Bridge
Rabindra Setu
Mullik Ghat
Flower Market
Howrah Train Station
Jagannath Ghat
Armenian Ghat
Eastern Railway Museum
Fairlie Ghat
BBD Bagh
Millennium Park
Botanical Gardens
Postal Museum
Writers' Building
Chintamony Dev Ghat
Bishe June Ghat
General Post Office
Metcalfe Hall
Mausolem of Job Charnock
Black Hole Memorial
St John's Church
Kiran Shankar Roy Rd
Kolkata Panorama
City Hall
Esplanade Row Went
Chandpal Ghat
Ferry Service
Babu Ghat
Raj Bhavan
Sahid Khudram Bose Rd
Netaji Indoor Stadium
Eden Gardens
Ranji Stadium, Eden Gardens
Eden Gardens
Statue of LBG Tilak
World War I Cenotaph
Outram Ghat
Princep Ferry Ghat
Eden Garden Road
Sahid Minar
Maidan
Fort William
Upper Foreshore Rd
Rishi Bankim Chandra Rd
N Mukherji Rd

Hooghly River

Lal Dighi
Hare St
BBD Bag S
BTM Sarani
Strand Rd
Fairlie Pl
BRN Mukherjee
Government Pl
Abdul Hamid St
Weston St
Marx Engels Beethi
Sido Kanhu Dahar
Esplanade
Government Rd

Howrah Bridge Road
Strand Bank Road
Strand Rd
Netaji Subhas Rd
Bazar Rd
Maharshi Debendra Rd
Hariram Goenka St
Kalakar St
Sibtala St
Tagore's House
Muktaram Babu St
Mahatma Gandhi Rd
Malulkalamani Gopabandhu Sarani
Bartala St
Marble Palace
Munsi Sadaruddi
Madari Mohan Burman St

Armenian Church
Armenian St
Nakhoda Mosque
Holy Rosary Cathedral
Amratala Ln
Moghan David Synagogue
Bethel Synagogue
Chinese Temples
Elephant Gateway
Old Chinatown
Bombay Safe
India Exchange
Old China
Biplabi Trailakya
Pollock St
Ezra St
St
St Andrew's Church
Maulana Saukat Ali St
Mahatma Gandhi Rd
BBD Bag N
BBD Bag St
Hemanta Basu Sarani
Lal Bazar St
B B Ganguly St
Central (North Exits)
Central (South Exits)
Ganesh
Chandni Chowk
Chittaranjan Ave
Chandni Chowk
Chandra St
Tippu Sultan's Mosque
Sacred Heart Church
Metropolitan Building
Lenin Sarani
Elite Cinema
Hospital St
Surrenda Nath Banerjee Rd
New Market
Market St
Chowringhee
Sudder St
Indian Museum
Marquis St
Collin St
Rafi Ahmed Kidwai Rd
Dr M D Ishaque Rd
Park Street
Kalanja Jama Masjid
Outram Rd
Victoria Memorial, Victoria Garden
Indira Gandhi Sarani
Dufferin Rd
Guru Nanak Sarani
Nehru Rd
Jawaharlal
Park St
Bertram St
Ghalib
Neli Sengupta Sarani

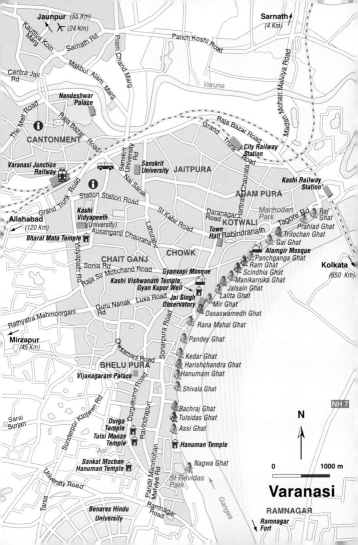

Jaunpur (55 Km)
(24 km)

Sarnath (4 Km)

Kautilya Koin Marg

Sarnath Rd.

Panch Koshi Road

Prem Chand Marg

Makbul Alam Marg

Madan Mohan Malviya Road

Centra Jail Rd.

Varuna

The Mail Road

Nandeshwar Palace

Raja Bazar Road

Raja Bazar Road

Grand Trunk Road

City Railway Station

CANTONMENT

Kashi Railway Station

Varanasi Junction Railway

Sanskrit University Rd

Sanskrit University

JAITPURA

Hartirat Chauraha

Nai Sarak

ADAM PURA

Grand Trunk Road

Station Road

Station Road

Si Kabir Road

Daranagar Road

Machodari Park

Tagore Rd.

Raj Ghat

Allahabad (120 Km)

Kashi Vidyapeeth (University)

Lahurabir

KOTWALI

Prahlad Ghat

Bharat Mata Temple

Ausanganji Chauraha

Town Hall

Rabindranath

Trilochan Ghat

Gai Ghat

CHAIT GANJ

Sonia Rd

CHOWK

Alamgir Mosque

Panchganga Ghat

Raja Sir Motichand Road

Vidyapeeth Rd

Gyanvapi Mosque

Ram Ghat

Kolkata (650 Km)

Scindhia Ghat

Kashi Vishwanath Temple, Gyan Kupor Well

Manikarnika Ghat

Guru Nanak Rd.

Luxa Road

Jai Singh Observatory

Jalsain Ghat

Lalita Ghat

Rathyatra Mahmoorgani

Mir Ghat

Mirzapur (45 Km)

Chitramani Road

Sonarpura Road

Dasaswamedh Ghat

Rana Mahal Ghat

Pandey Ghat

BHELU PURA

Kedar Ghat

Harishchandra Ghat

Vijanagaram Palace

Hanumam Ghat

Durgakund Road

Ravindrapur

Shivala Ghat

Bachraj Ghat

Sunderpur Klojwan Rd.

Durga Temple

Tulsi Manas Temple

Tulsidas Ghat

Assi Ghat

N

Sarai Surjan

Ravindrapur

Hanuman Temple

NH 7

Sankat Mochan Hanuman Temple

Pandit Manmohan Malviya Rd

Nagwa Ghat

0   1000 m

University Road

St Ravidas Park

Tania

Benares Hindu University

Ramnagar Road

Ganges

Varanasi

RAMNAGAR

Ramnagar Fort

NEPAL

Kathmandu! The name alone summons images of the exotic, adventurous and remote. Such words accurately describe Nepal even today.

Much of the population of this country, open to foreign visitors only since 1951, lives in villages reached by days of climbing mountain trails. But Kathmandu, the valley capital at the foot of the Himalayas, concentrating the essence of Nepali customs and culture, is within easy reach of the most comfort-conscious traveller.

The approach from the south by air is spectacular. First you fly over jungles and the narrow lowland strip, the Terai, that adjoins India, then the brown wall of the Mahabarat Range. The highest part of the Himalayas, including the peak of Mount Everest, embraces the horizon. Abruptly, your pilot swoops down into the

wide bowl of Kathmandu Valley, green in summer, gold in autumn, as the rice sprouts and matures.

In the valley, you'll get three cities for the price of one: Kathmandu, the seat of the democratic parliament with its Old Town maze of palaces, temples and markets; rose-red Patan of the golden roofs just across the Bagmati River; and medieval Bhaktapur (Bhadgaon), a city of artisans 10 km (6 miles) to the east. Each has outstanding monuments of architecture and art. A short drive or bicycle ride from Kathmandu's centre are major shrines dating back 1,500 years, as well as villages where rural life styles have not changed in centuries. About

200 km (125 miles) west of Kathmandu is Pokhara, the country's second city, a base for trekkers tackling the Annapurna Circuit.

Whenever you visit, you're bound to witness colourful rituals of Hinduism, the faith of eight out of ten Nepalis. But some of the most impressive temples and festivals are Bhuddist, and the people of Kathmandu are remarkably impartial in revering holy sites, figures and celebrations of both religions.

Namaste, the welcoming greeting is suitable for kings and commoners alike. It is said with both hands at breast level in an upright prayer position. It means "I salute the divine in you."

A BRIEF HISTORY

4th–8th centuries
The Licchavi Hindu dynasty rules the valley, converts to Buddhism and expands control of Nepal at the expense of the Indian emperors.

13th–17th centuries
Following Muslim conquest of northern India, a refugee Hindu prince from Rajasthan founds the Malla dynasty and restores Hindu dominance. In 1336 the Muslim Sultan of Bengal raids Kathmandu Valley, destroying Hindu and Buddhist temples in seven days. Swayambunath and Pashupatinath are rebuilt and expanded to their present form. Upon the death of King Yaksha Malla in 1482, the land is divided among his heirs.

18th–19th centuries
Prithvi Narayan Shah, "The Great", Prince of Ghorka, captures Kathmandu and Patan in 1768 and Bhaktapur a year later. He extends his rule into India and Tibet. The British invade from India in 1814 and are beaten back by soldiers from Gorkha, earning all Nepali fighting men fierce reputation as "Gurkhas". In a second invasion two years later, the British recover Sikkim and Darjeeling and establish the present borders of Nepal. In 1846 Jung Bahadur Rana becomes first in the line of hereditary prime ministers who control Nepal for 104 years, keeping out foreigners and building palaces in Kathmandu.

20th century–present
In 1950 and 51, after Indian independence, opposition to Rana rule builds. The puppet king escapes to India. After the uprising, prime minister Mohan Shumshere Rana resigns, the king returns and a first constitution is adopted. King Birendra accedes to the throne in 1972. A new constitution is installed in 1990 allowing multi-party elections. The next year the Nepali Congress Party wins a narrow majority over Communists in the new parliament. The king becomes a constitutional monarch. In 2001, the Crown Prince Dipendra massacres the king, queen and all direct heirs to the throne, including himself. Birendra's brother Gyanendra accedes to the throne. Maoist insurgents cause widespread disruption. After violent protests the parliament reconvenes for the first time in four years in 2006. At the end of 2007 the parliament declares a democratic, federally organized Republic; it is accepted in May 2008 and the monarchy is abolished.

On the Scene

Take a deep breath and plunge into Old Kathmandu, the inner core of the capital founded in the 8th century.

Kathmandu

The most direct route from the hotel area is down **Kanti Path**, the broad avenue lined on the west with former palaces of the despotic Rana family, and on the east with a large open-air market and the Tundikhel parade ground. Ahead you'll see the Bhimsen Tower, a useful reference point whenever you need to get your bearings. But before you reach the tower, turn west on **New Road**, a commercial street leading to Old Kathmandu's gateway, **Durbar Square**.

Durbar means palace. The red-brick **Hanuman Dhoka Durbar** is the centrepiece of a spectacular cluster of pagoda temples, shrines and statues. The palace was the residence of Malla kings from the 16th century on, but now it is mainly a museum, also used for coronations and certain royal devotions. An effigy of Hanuman, the Hindu monkey god stands by the main door, caked with offerings of red powder. Guides claim that the powder prevents Hanuman from seeing the erotic antics carved on the lower struts of the facing small **Jaganath Temple**. Just inside the entrance, note the 1673 sculpture of Vishnu as Narasingha, the man-lion, disembowelling a demon. A great view over the old city is offered from the upper storeys of the palace's **Basantapur Tower**. One wing is dedicated to a museum of miscellaneous mundane objects, such as a phonograph and bicycle that belonged to King Birendra's grandfather, King Tribhuvan.

To the left of the palace is the **Basantapur Chowk**, a raised open space that used to house the royal elephants. Now curio vendors spread their wares on the bricks —human skull bowls, tortoise shell face maks, Tibetan prayer wheels, brass "singing bowls" that ring and a thousand other strange artefacts.

A bit farther on is the **Kasthamandap**, an open-sided structure made from the wood of a single tree. The word means "House of Wood" and may be the origin of Kathmandu's name. Adjoining is a Ganesh shrine polished by the hands of passers-by who touch it or ring its bells for good luck.

Few Kathmandu streets are signposted. The lane leading left from Basantapur Chowk earned the name "**Freak Street**" in the 1960s when western hippies flocked here for cheap drugs. Narcotics have been banned since 1973, and Freak Street now purveys trekking gear and Nepali vests and jackets.

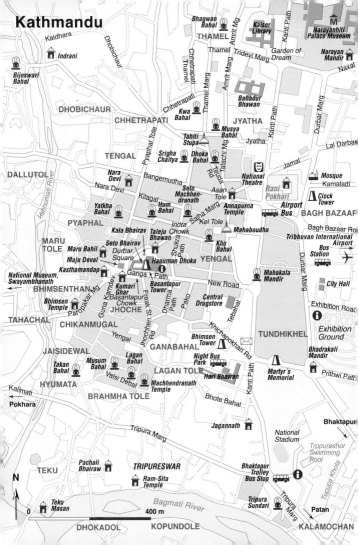

Kathmandu

Kaldhara

Indrani

Bijeswari
Bahal

DHOBICHAUR

DALLUTOL

Dhobichaur

Chhetrapati

Thamel Chhetrapati

CHHETRAPATI

Bhagwan
Bahal

THAMEL

Kaiser
Library

Thamel Tridevi Marg

Garden of
Dream

Narayanhiti
Palace Museum

Narayan
Mandir

Naxal

TENGAL

Nara
Devi

Nara Devi

Pyaphal Tole

Bangemudha

Tahiti
Stupa

Srigha
Chaitya

Kwa
Bahal

Musya
Bahal

Dhoka
Bahal

JYATHA

Jyatha

Kanti Path

Kanti Path

Durbar Marg

Lal Darba

Bahadur
Bhawan

Mosque
Kamaladi

PYAPHAL

Yatkha
Bahal

Kilagat

Hum
Bahal

Seto
Machhen-
dranath

Seto Bhairav

Asan
Tole

Salha Marg

Annapurna
Temple

Kel Tole

Mahaboudha

National
Theatre

Rani
Pokhari

Clock
Tower

Airport
Bus

BAGH BAZAAR

Bagh Bazaar Ro

MARU
TOLE

Maru Bahil

Maju Deval

Kala Bhairav

Taleju
Bhawan

Durbar
Square

Indra
Chowk

Shukra
Path

Hanuman Dhoka

Khu
Bahal

YENGAL

Tribhuvan International
Airport

Bus
Station

Kasthamandap

Ganga
Path

Basantapur
Tower

New Road

Mahakala
Mandir

City Hall

National Museum,
Swayambhunath

BHIMSENTHAN

Bhimsen
Temple

TAHACHAL

Guna Kamdev

Patonakari Mg

Kumari
Ghar

Basantapura
Chowk

Dharma
Path

Pako

Central
Drugstore

Tebahal

Exhibition Road

CHIKANMUGAL

JHOCHE

Freak St Jhochen Rd

Tebahal

Khichapokhari Rd

TUNDHIKHEL

Exhibition
Ground

Bhadrakali
Mandir

JAISIDEWAL

Yengal

GANABAHAL

Bhimsen
Tower

Prithwi Marg

HYUMATA

Takan
Bahal

Musum
Bahal

Valsi Debal

Lagan
Bahal

LAGAN TOLE

Machhendranath
Temple

Night Bus
Park

Hari Bhawan

Kanti Path

Martyr's
Memorial

Kalimati

Pokhara

BRAHMHA TOLE

Bhote Bahal

TEKU

Pachali
Bhairaw

TRIPURESWAR

Jagannath

Tripura Marg

Ram-Sita
Temple

Bagmati River

N

Teku
Masan

0

400 m

DHOKADOL

KOPUNDOLE

Bhaktapur

National
Stadium

Tropureshor
Swimming
Pool

Bhaktapur
Trolley
Bus Stop

Tripura
Sundari

Tripura Marg

Tucuca Khola

Patan

Bhaktapur

KALAMOCHAN

Straight on past the curio sellers is the house of the **Kumari**, a girl-child regarded as the living reincarnation of the goddess Parvati. The Kumari's job is to protect Kathmandu and its citizens. Seven times a year she is carried through the streets on a litter. The rest of the time, from about age four to puberty, when she loses her divinity and another child replaces her, she must stay inside her house. You may get a glimpse of her heavily made-up face from an upstairs window if enough visitors come to her courtyard and make contributions.

Return to Durbar Square, where several pagoda temples face the palace. The first is to Vishnu and is guarded by a kneeling Garuda. In the centre is Shiva's **Maju Deval** pagoda, its broad steps usually draped with people photographing the smiling painted effigies of Shiva and Parvati leaning out of a window of the adjoining temple. The huge bell here and the giant drums a bit further on were used to summon the populace to the palace for important announcements.

Pigeons are plentiful and fat in the Kathmandu Valley, profiting from the daily ritual that every Nepali observes of *puja*, or offerings to the gods of rice, grain, oil or marigold petals. A cloud of them flutters around the **Kala** (black) **Bhairav** shrine outside the palace, a very popular site sacred to this brightly painted, black-limbed *avatar* (meaning "different form") of destroying Shiva. Criminals once were interrogated here because it was believed that anyone telling a lie before Bhairav would bleed to death. A **Seto** (white) **Bhairav** rewards worshippers during the *Indra Jatra* festival by spouting beer from a lacquered mask set behind a latticed window in a nearby wall.

As you shoulder your way through Durbar Square you'll be jostled by bearded *sadhus* (holy beggars), and women from the countryside lugging baskets of vegetables. Bicycle bells and rickshaw horns will make you jump, your path may be suddenly blocked by a herd of goats or a procession following a flower-decked image on a chariot. An elephant may glide by on its soundless, almost floating padded gait.

Beyond the palace the scene becomes even more congested and bewildering. This is the beginning of Old Kathmandu's most colourful, busiest shopping street, leading back to the Kanti Path at the National Theatre and *Rani Pokhari* (Queen's Pond) basin.

From the Durbar Square area, the first intersection is **Indra Chowk**, where four dragon-lions stand guard by a stairway to a bal-

The all-seeing eyes of Buddha at the Bodnath stupa.

conied building. The next junction is **Kel Tole**, where an entrance on the left leads into the courtyard of the **Seto Machendranath Temple**. Machendranath is a popular Buddhist Bodhisattva, or saint. His temple displays not only Buddhist prayer wheels but also Hindu images, an example of Kathmandu's unique blending of religions.

The busiest of all the intersections comes next, **Asan Tole**. This is an important marketing place where rice is sold in bulk, porters stand about waiting for work, vegetables are heaped on the pavement, housewives haggle, loose cows scavenge for leaves and cyclists shout warnings as they weave through the crowds. The burnished brass shrine here is to **Annapurna**, goddess of abundance.

Turn left at Asan Tole and head north to **Tahitty Tole**, an entrance to the bustling **Thamel** district.

Thamel's international restaurants, pleasant small hotels and guest houses are popular with young people, trekkers and budget-conscious visitors. This is the place to rent bicycles, plan a trek at a specialized agency or scan bulletin boards for second-hand gear or a trekking partner.

The Tridevi Marg from Thamel's centre passes the tall trees hung by day with the dark, pendulous shapes of fruit bats and at twilight crowded with chattering birds. Behind the trees, the **Kaiser Library**, in the Ministry of Education affords a glimpse into a former Rana Palace filled with photographs of family members posed with tigers and other game they shot in Nepal's Chitwan jungle. After the library, across Kanti Path, flagpoles bearing the world's only non-rectangular flag mark the **Narayanhiti Royal Palace Museum**, the former home of the royal family.

The broad avenue leading south from the palace gate is Kathmandu's modern centre — **Durbar Marg**. There are always taxis and motorized rickshaws called *tempos* waiting here and to the right down Jamal Street at the Rani Pokhari and Kanti Path.

Patan

Almost a suburb of Kathmandu, south over the river, Patan is so far from the present as to be a living museum, its monuments among the finest and best preserved in all Nepal. In the narrow lanes and rose-hued temple-lined squares, life goes on as it has for centuries. Patan was the capital of one of the kingdoms created in 1482 when King Yaksha Malla divided his territory into three parts for his three sons. It was known then as Lalitpur, "Lovely City"; its official name today is Lalitpur Sub-Metropolitan City.

In **Durbar Square**, no fewer than eight temples cluster round the **Deotalli Durbar** palace. In the middle, a golden statue of King Yoganarendra Malla (1648 –1705) sits on a throne on top of a column, sheltered by the hood of a giant cobra on which a bronze bird is perched. Legend has it that as long as this bird and others like it on the roof corners of temples do not fly away, the king's spirit will abide in the valley.

Several of the temples in the square are spires of Indian inspiration. One, the **Krishna Mandir** built in 1636, is of stone, a relative rarity in Nepal. Friezes running around the two lower storeys depict scenes from the great Hindu epics, the *Mhabarata* and *Ramayana*. These images keep the sacred histories alive for illiterate devotees. A golden Garuda in his usual *namaste* pose kneels on a pillar in front of his master's temple.

The low, tile-roofed palace of dark red brick is built around three interior courtyards. Note the luxurious sunken royal tub, decorated with sculpted gods and snakes, in the first, the **Sundari Chowk**. The larger **Mul Chowk** boasts very fine bronze reliefs of the goddesses Ganga (standing on a crocodile) and Jamuna (on a tortoise). The representation over a doorway here of the sun god, Surya, driving a chariot and seven-horse team, offers an intriguing parallel with the Greek Apollo myth. An even more beautiful panel called the **Golden Gate** above the sealed outer doorway to the third courtyard honours Shiva and his Parvati.

Amid this opulence, the alleys and lanes of Patan resemble those of a country village, where families are hard at work, washing, weaving, drying grain and chillies on mats before their doorsteps. These lanes, too, lead past abandoned temples with grass sprouting from their tiles, to hidden treasures, such as the **Kwa Bahal** off Durbar Square where two white-painted lions flank the otherwise unobtrusive gate. This 11th century Buddhist monastery is still in use. It is renowned for the exquisite **Golden Temple**, a shrine in its central courtyard that photographers adore.

The main street passing Durbar Square continues to the tall

Mahaboudha, or Temple of the Thousand Buddhas. Each of the bricks and tiles on the four faces of this 16th century spire bears an image of Buddha.

Bhaktapur

The atmosphere of Bhaktapur is even more medieval than Patan or Old Kathmandu. The town occupies a valley slope some 16 km (10 miles) east of the capital, surrounded by the fields of Newar farmers. It, too, was once the seat of a kingdom and has its Malla dynasty palace, the **Tripura Durbar**, or Palace of 55 Windows, begun in the 15th century and enlarged in the 18th century by King Bhupatindra Malla. The king looks down on his handi-work from a pillar in Durbar Square. The main entrance *torana* (a semi-circular panel often found over doorways) is famed as the **Sun Dhoka**, another "Golden Gate". The ten-armed goddess in its centre is Taleju, an avatar of Parvati and protector of the royal family. The Taleju temple inside is closed to non-Hindus but there is an adjoining art museum notable for its collection of *thangkas* ("wheel-of-life" paintings).

At the far end of Durbar Square is a temple to **Durga**, embellished by pairs of sculpted animals on its stairs. Empty platforms in the square are the sites of temples destroyed in the earthquake of 1934 which hit Bhaktapur hardest. Many of the city's

---

Flights. Everybody wants to see Mount Everest, at 8,848 m (29,028 ft) the top of the world. Several companies organize thrilling hour-long flights taking you close to the peak and along a stretch of the snowy Himalayas with 19 mountains over 6,000 m (18,000 ft). The Himalayas were formed 60 million years ago when the Indian subcontinent, then a drifting island, collided with Asia and forced up what had been part of the Tibetan plateau.

Flights leave every morning when the weather is good. The pilot invites passengers into the cockpit two at a time to photograph. It doesn't matter which side of the plane you sit on, for you'll get a different view coming back. Every passenger gets a profile of the range to help identify 19 top peaks, including the four Annapurnas, Kanchenjunga, Dhaulagiri, Manaslu and Macchapuchare, the "fishtail" mountain called Nepal's Matterhorn.

Everest has been climbed over 5,000 times since Sir Edmund Hillary and Sherpa Tenzing Norgay first reached the summit in 1953. Two sherpas have climbed five times the peak they call Sagarmatha, "Mother of the Universe". The first woman to the top (in 1975) was Japanese.

monuments have been, or are still being, restored in cooperation between Nepali and western experts, making use of the traditional skills of local craftsmen. These artisans can be seen at work all over town.

Behind a 15th-century version of the Pashupatinath temple on Durbar Square, a short street goes down to **Taumadi Tole** and the **Nyatapola Temple**, a five-tiered pagoda. Two Malla wrestlers and pairs of animals in ascending order of strength line the steps up to the doorway. It hasn't been opened since the temple was built in 1702 and no one knows what may be inside.

Wander through back streets to Bhaktapur's oldest square, **Tachupal Tole**. You'll recognize it by the burly wrestler statues and a golden Garuda kneeling on a column in front of the **Dattatraya Temple** used by both Hindus and Bhuddists. Just off this square is the carved wood **Peacock Window** in an upper storey of the Pujahari Math, once a priest's house and now a government office.

Three Amazing Temples

The hilltop temple of **Swayambunath** (also called the Monkey Temple) is the seat of the Chinia Lama, a Tibetan dignitary. Its golden tower is an instantly recognizable symbol that can be seen from afar. Take a taxi to the base of the hill west of the city and follow the pilgrim path up 365 statue-lined steps through a wooded park to the temple platform. Look out for monkeys that love to snatch anything loose. Have some coins ready for the outstretched hands of old women sitting by the steps.

The white mound *(stupa)* at the base of the shrine is at least 2,000 years old. Above it rises a golden cube bearing on four sides the rather angry-looking "all-seeing" eyes of Buddha. The "nose" is actually the Nepali numeral "one", signifying the one true path. Above the cube is a golden cone formed by 13 progressively smaller disks that represent Buddhism's 13 steps to enlightenment. This is topped by a gold royal parasol and bell-shaped crown from which brightly coloured prayer flags flutter on cords from the base. All day long, pilgrims walk round the base, spinning the row of prayer wheels that encircle the stupa.

A **Tibetan Monastery** near the stairs can be visited. At 4 p.m. you'll hear drums and cymbals and the deep moan of the long horns blown by monks in their red and gold chapel. Nearby is a large *dorje* thunderbolt symbol on a pedestal and two Indian-style *shikara* towers dedicated to Hindu deities. The platform is covered with images and small white votive shrines. Sunset, when Swayambunath's tower glows a red-gold, is a magical time to visit and view the valley and city below.

The **National Museum**, between Kathmandu and Swayambunath, is a good place to get the relationship between art and religion in perspective. It has a small but choice collection of art from some of the valley's 2,500 temples.

The Buddhist shrine of **Bodnath**, a short way from Kathmandu on the side opposite Swayambunath, is not to be missed. The white-domed *stupa* surmounted by a golden tower is on the flat, surrounded by a compound of *gompas* (Tibetan monasteries), pilgrims' lodges and shops. You come upon it suddenly as you emerge from a narrow passage. The all-seeing eyes seem even more penetrating than those of Swayambunath. The flag-decked dome and tower loom with great power above the slow-moving procession of pilgrims ever turning the prayer wheels set in the stupa's base. Here you can climb up on the dome on stairs between painted cement elephants.

One of the most sacred spots for all Hindus is the great temple complex of **Pashupatinath** on the Bagmati River, not far from Bodnath toward the airport. It is the principal shrine to Shiva, patron of Nepal, in his avatar of Pashu-pati, Lord of the Beasts. Non-Hindus can approach the temple down an alley of shops selling tea and the makings of offerings to the god, but they may not enter.

From the bridge you can look down on the burning ghats where most of Kathmandu's Hindu dead are cremated. There is usually a cremation under way, the body resting on a pyre of wood. Afterwards, the ashes are scattered in the river, which is a tributary of the Ganges and therefore holy. The faithful take purification baths in the less-than-pure Bagmati during the many religious festivals held throughout the year.

Around Kathmandu Valley

Many interesting places in the valley can be visited in a few hours by tour bus, taxi, bicycle or by a leisurely walk. Rice paddies and rural villages where life follows age-old patterns are just minutes away from the centre of town. You'll see rice being threshed and winnowed by hand, water buffalo harnessed to the plough, pumpkin vines growing over Newar farm rooftops and maybe chickens roosting in an upstairs window.

A raucous Nepali gathering occurs on Saturdays and most Tuesdays at **Dakshinkali**, a Hindu shrine to Kali at the southern end of the valley. Families come out to sacrifice chickens and goats to

Kali, then consume the offerings at barbecues by the banks of a stream while loudspeakers blare hymns to the goddess.

Pharping, Bungamati, Thecho and Chapagaon are places to see village life. **Kirtipur** is the fourth-largest town in the valley, noted for textiles woven by women on hand looms that clatter from the doorways of the houses. Among several notable Kirtipur monuments, the **Bagh Bhairav Temple** in the centre of town is hung with swords and shields captured during the 18th-century siege by Prithvi the Great, unifier of Nepal.

North of Kathmandu, great views of the Himalayas may be seen at **Nagarkot**. You can spend the night here and at Dhulikhel, farther west, to watch sunset and sunrise gild the top of the world.

Other notable valley landmarks are the reclining Vishnu at **Buddhanilkantha**, 8 km (5 miles) north of the capital, and the fascinating temple at **Changu Narayan**, a short distance north of Bhaktapur. This is the oldest in the district, with masterpieces dating back to the 5th century. You can even sample trekking on a day's hike from Budhanilkantha up Shivapuri Peak and ride elephants to see the tigers in the Safari Park at Gokarna. The park provides transportation to and from Kathmandu hotels just half an hour away.

Pokhara

Frequent buses run from Kathmandu to Nepal's second city, with a population of 251,000. It is located within 50 km (30 miles) of three of the world's ten highest mountains: Dhaulagiri, Annapurna I and Manaslu. Pokhara lies on an old trading route between China and India and could be reached only on foot until the end of the 1960s. Since the first road was built in 1968, the city grew rapidly, thanks to tourism and notably trekkers on their way to or from Annapurna Base Camp and Mustang. The shops, small hotels, restaurants and bars aimed at tourists spread along the shore of Phewa Lake west of the centre, in areas known as Baidam, Lakeside and Damside. For good views of the area climb up to the **World Peace Pagoda** (1996) by the trail marked with peace signs, from Damside—or take a taxi, which will leave you within 15 minutes' walk of the pagoda.

In town, you can visit the **International Mountain Museum** to learn more about the people of the Himalayas, or the **Gurkha Memorial Museum** dedicated to Nepal's famous soldiers. The **Annapurna Natural History Museum** displays local flora, fauna and especially a collection of butterflies.

North of the city is **Mahendra Cave**, with stalagmites, stalactites and plenty of bats, with more of these creatures clinging to the walls of **Chamare Gufa**, Bat Cave, 10 minutes' walk away.

Dining Out

The national dish is *dhal baat*, a spicy mixture of lentils, rice, some greens and hot peppers eaten together in a bowl. Kathmandu has several good restaurants serving regional specialities. From Tibet come *gyakok*, a "chimney pot" fondue of meat and vegetables in rich broth; *momos*, tasty fried or steamed dumplings filled with minced pork, garlic and cabbage; and a noodle soup called *miso*. You'll also find Indian curries and chicken tandoori.

Durbar Marg has several international restaurants, and there are lively and inexpensive eateries in the Thamel district. Because they cater to foreigners, many of these kitchens announce that they boil and filter water and sterilize vegetables. This is really important. Kathmandu in general is not big on hygiene.

Shopping

Kathmandu is the proverbial "shopper's paradise." Prices are reasonable and workmanship is excellent. You often can buy from artisans in their workshops.

Curios on sale include *kukris*, the curved daggers of the Gurkhas, brass singing bowls, silver-lined wooden tea bowls, hand-painted masks, enamelled and inlaid boxes and figures of gods, animals and birds. Around Freak Street you'll find tailors making warm wool red and black waistcoats and jackets and caps. The stretch of street from the palace to the Indra Chowk intersection is Old Kathmandu's centre for copper and brass pots, sari fabrics, the colourful *topi* caps worn by Newar men. Look for hand-knit sweaters, socks and mittens, cashmere shawls and pashminas.

Durbar Marg is for upscale shops, antiques and jewellery. The Mahaguthi Shop just off this street has a selection of handicrafts from different parts of Nepal. It is a cooperative run for the benefit of rural women.

Go to the Industrial Estate on the far side of Patan to visit the workshops of woodcarvers and bronze casters.

Bhaktapur is famed for paintings, including *thangkas*. The Bodnath temple compound is the place for Tibetan prayer wheels, copper temple horns, drums, fur hats and other objects brought by pilgrims to pay for their trip from Tibet. You will also find stalls selling similar goods at the Tibetan settlement near the airport at Pokhara.

PRACTICAL INFORMATION

Banks. Open Sunday to Thursday 10 a.m.–2.30 p.m., Fridays 10 a.m.–noon. A special foreign exchange counter of Nepal Bank Ltd. in New Road opens Sunday to Thursday 10 a.m.–3 p.m. and Fridays 10 a.m.–noon. Money may also be changed at Tribhuvan airport, at hotels and travel agencies authorized by the state. Keep receipts when you change money, and change only small amounts at a time. Hotel and airline bills must be paid in hard currency, preferably US dollars.

Climate. The best time to visit is October–November when the hot, humid and rainy June-September monsoon has passed and the climate turns balmy. Cold temperatures in December–February are compensated by cloudless skies. March and April, when the rhododendrons bloom, are popular, too.

Currency. The Nepal *rupee* (Rs.) is divided into 100 *paisa*. Coins range from 5 to 50 paisa, and 1 to 5 rupees; banknotes from 1 to 1000 rupees. Indian rupees are accepted in Nepal and can easily be changed.

Credit cards. Only American Express is widely accepted.

Electricity. 220 volts. There are frequent power cuts.

Health. Bottled water, tea, soft drinks and beer are safe; water is not, except in the better hotels. Steer clear of "atmospheric" eateries in Old Kathmandu. Shots or boosters for cholera, polio, typhoid-tetanus and gamma globulin for hepatitis resistance are recommended.

Hours. Shops open around 9 a.m. and close at 7 p.m. or later. Public offices and some shops are closed on Saturdays. International offices usually shut Saturday and Sunday.

Post offices. The General Post Office on Kanti Path is open Sunday to Thursday 10 a.m.–5 p.m., Fridays 10 a.m.–3 p.m. The big hotels also have a postal service.

Telephone. International telephone connections are improving. The outgoing access code is 00.

Time. UTC/GMT + 5.45.

Tipping. Avoid tipping, except in hotels, restaurants and for helpful taxi drivers, when 10% is customary.

BHUTAN

High in the eastern Himalayas, Bhutan is a small, mysterious country; many think of it as the last Shangri-La. It is landlocked by China beyond the mountains to the north and India to the south, where the forests of the centre give way to tropical lowland.

About 350 km (218 miles) from east to west, and 150 km (93 miles) from north to south, it is home to 670,000 people. Flying into Paro, the country's only airport, by plane, you will skim over steep valleys and lush crops, past tiny villages and sacred monasteries. An hour by road to the east is the fast-growing capital, Thimphu, with 90,000 inhabitants.

Throughout its history, Bhutanese society has changed very little. Most people have always been subsistence farmers, exploiting the rugged land but living in harmony with the pristine natural environment. Today, 75 per cent of the population still live in rural Bhutan. Separated by high mountain ridges, the sparsely scattered communities survived independently, evolving distinct cultural traits, spiritual beliefs, traditional clothing, and even their own language groups. Only since the 1960s has there been significant progress in their lives with the construction of infrastructures such as roads, schools and hospitals, limited modernization of the agricultural system and the introduction of a communications network. Today Bhutan is poised to enter a new era of change, as the king, like his father before him, is keen to let the people have their say in its destiny. The issues are complex as the country tries to reconcile rapid urbanization with the survival of spiritual legacies while attempting to maintain rural traditions.

Snow-fed rapids and foamy waterfalls punctuate the long range of majestic snow-capped peaks. The deep, lush valleys are terraced with rice fields or carpeted with wild flowers, in an outburst of colours. Trekkers can travel through quiet countryside for days, with only the numerous wild animals and birds that thrive in this beautiful habitat for company.

A BRIEF HISTORY

Early times

Stone tools indicate the settlement of Bhutan more than 4,000 years ago. The first known leaders are religious figures. In the 7th century King Songtsen Gampo of Tibet commissions 108 monasteries to be built in the Himalayan region, and two of them are located in Bhutan. A century later Guru Rinpoche (Padmasambhava) lays the foundations of the Buddhist heritage. Lamas fleeing persecution in Tibet establish monastic orders.

17th–19th centuries

Zhabdrung Ngawang Namgyal, a dynamic spiritual and military leader who comes to Bhutan from Tibet in 1616, unifies the country and introduces the dual system of rule by spiritual and temporal heads. Repeated Tibetan invasions are repelled. The Zhabdrung is acknowledged as the architect of the Bhutanese national identity, having developed the sociocultural legacy that still exists today. A turbulent period of power struggles among regional chieftains follows. In the 18th and 19th centuries, Bhutanese forces twice occupy neighbouring parts of northern India but are expelled by British colonial troops. In 1865 Bhutan and Britain sign a treaty defining the border.

20th century–present

Having defeated his rivals for power, Gongsar Ugyen Wangchuck is elected in 1907 as the first hereditary monarch. The rule of four successive kings of the Wangchuck dynasty is marked by relative peace and stability. The third king, Jigme Dorji Wangchuck, initiates the process of planned modernization and is often referred to as the father of modern Bhutan. The fourth ruler Jigme Singye Wangchuck, is credited with the phenomenal development of the late 20th century. The first five-year development plan is started in 1961. By the end of the century the political system is democratized. Jigme Singye abdicates in favour of his son, Jigme Kesar Namgyal, in 2006. In March 2008, the first parliamentary elections are held, won by the DPT party, marking the end of the transition towards a constitutional monarchy. Tourism is cautiously encouraged, but the main hope for future prosperity is the generation and export to India of hydro-electric power.

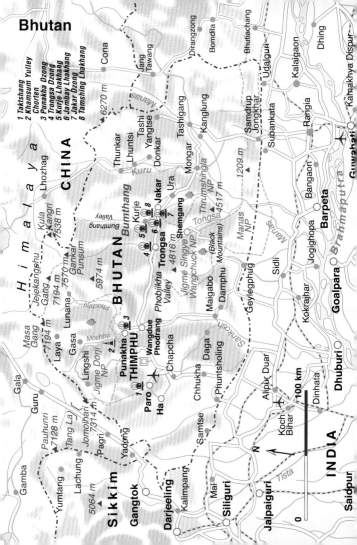

Bhutan

1 Taktshang
2 Khamsum Yulley
3 Chorten
4 Punakha Dzong
5 Kurje Lhakhang
6 Jambay Lhakhang
7 Jakar Dzong
8 Tamshing Lhakhang

CHINA

Himalaya

BHUTAN

INDIA

Sikkim

Cona
Jang
Tawang
Dirangzong
Bomdila
Bhutiachang
Dhing
Udalguri
Kalaigaon
Kamakhya Dispur

Thunkar
Lhuntsi
Tashi
Yangtse
Donkar
Mongar
Tashigang
Kanglung
Samdrup
Jongkhar
Subankata
Rangia
Guwahati

6270 m
Kuru

Kula
Kangri
7538 m

Gankar
Punsum
7570 m

5974 m

Jakar
Ura
8
7
Kurje
5
6
4
Trongsa
Shemgang

Bumthang
Valley

Thrumshingla
NP
4517 m

1209 m

Bangaon
Barpeta

Jigme Singye
Wangchuck NP
4816 m

(Black
Mountains)
Tongsa
Manas
NP

Jogighopa
Goalpara
Brahmaputra

Masa
Gang
7194 m

Jejekangshu
Gang
7194 m

Phochu

Lunana

Gasa

Mochhu

Punakha
2
3
THIMPHU
Wangdue
Phodrang
Chapcha

Phobjikha
Valley

Maigabo
Damphu

Jigme Dorji
NP

Lingshi

Laya

Daga

Samkosh

Geylegphug
Sidli
Manas
NP

Kokrajhar
Goalpara

Dhuburi

Gala
Guru

Pauhunri
7128 m

Tang La

Jomolhari
7314 m

Yadong

Pagri

Masa
Gang

1
Paro
Ha

Chhukha
Phuntsholing
Samtse

Alipur Duat
Koch
Bihar
Dinhata

Gamba
Yumtang
Lachung

5064 m

Gangtok
Darjeeling
Kalimpang
Mal
Siliguri
Jalpaiguri
Saidpur

Tista

N

100 km

0

On the Scene

The sense of changing times is palpable in Bhutan, but there are many ancient, sacred monuments to visit.

Thimphu

If most of Bhutan seems to be living in another age, Thimphu, 2,320 m (7,610 ft) above sea level, bubbles with activity—new construction, busy shops, hordes of children trooping to school.

Built in 1744 and expanded over the centuries, **Tashichhodzong** is a commanding monastic fortress on the northern outskirts. The throne room of the Druk Gyalpo (King) and residence of the Je Khenpo (chief abbot) are housed in the *dzong*, which is also the seat of national governance, shared by the government and the monastic order, comprising 1,500 monks. All year long it is busy with religious ceremonies and prayers, high-level government meetings, and lively religious dance festivals, *tshechu* and *drubchhen* held in autumn.

Near the centre of the town, the **National Memorial Chhorten** (stupa) is a monument to the third king of Bhutan, adorned with tantric art representing images of Vajrayana Buddhism, the dominant spiritual practice. The faithful walk round it, chanting, murmuring mantras and spinning prayer wheels.

The **National Library** is a reservoir of scriptures, documented mostly in the classical text known as *Chhoekey*, and *Dzongkha*, Bhutan's national language. The collections include rare and ancient scriptures printed from woodblocks (xielography), and there's a good selection of books on Buddhism and Himalayan culture. One of the world's biggest books, *Bhutan—A Visual Odyssey across the Kingdom*, measuring 150 by 210 cm (5 by 7 ft), is also on display.

The **Textile Museum** showcases the best-known of Bhutan's traditional handicrafts, the ancient art of weaving. In households and villages in remote eastern Bhutan, this brings a valuable income to many women who labour for hours over their handlooms producing intricate, colourful fabrics. The museum organizes an annual textile festival and national weaving competition in autumn.

The **Folk Heritage Museum** is a restored three-storey traditional farmhouse, equipped with the household furniture, tools and farm implements that would have been used in the past—and in many cases are still in use today.

The inhabitants of Thimphu gather every weekend at the **vegetable market**, a bustling place also selling fruit, meat, handicrafts, household utensils and farm tools, as well as imported cloth-

Taktshang Monastery, clinging to the cliffside, is a veritable technical achievement.

ing. It begins on Friday evening, when the farmers from outlying villages bring in their produce, and remains open until Sunday evening. The best times to visit are Saturday or Sunday morning when the local people do their food shopping. Follow your nose to the seasonal attractions such as exotic mushrooms in many varieties and local cheeses in varying degrees of fermentation, and mountains of chillies. The handicrafts section is a particularly good place to hunt for unusual souvenirs such as hand-turned wooden bowls, textiles, incense, bamboo bows and arrows, and religious instruments. You'll hear people trying out trumpets and cymbals before they make a purchase.

The **Takin Reserve** on a wooded hillside to the west of Thimphu is home to some examples of the national animal, the rare takin. Like a cross between a goat and an antelope, but bigger and stockier, it roams the mountains of Tibet and Nepal as well as Bhutan.

Around Bhutan

From Thimphu you can drive and then walk up to numerous **monasteries** perched on ridges on both sides of the valley. The Phajoding, Tango, Cheri, and Dechenphu monasteries as well as the Semtokha dzong are all centres of Buddhist studies that include advanced meditation courses for monks. A visit to these monasteries is memorable, not only for the sacred atmosphere but also for the enjoyable trek through the forests.

At 2,280 m (7,480 ft), the scenic valley of **Paro** abounds in spiritual sites, while its fertile farmland has made its people among the most prosperous in the country. As well as Bhutans airport, it has a number of hotels and a couple of luxury resorts.

The sacred monastery of **Kyichu Lhakhang** is one of two commissioned by Songtsen Gampo, king of Tibet, in the 7th century. It predates the introduction of Buddhism by the popular saint, Guru Rinpoche (Padmasambhava), in the 8th century.

The seat of the Paro clergy and district administration, the imposing **Rinpung Dzong** fortress-monastery is best known for its spring festival, the Paro Tshechu. This four-day religious dance celebration draws a big crowd of tourists every year but still retains a traditional atmosphere. One of the highlights, early in the morning on the last day, is the unfurling of a giant *thoengdrel* (silk tapestry) against one side of the *dzong*.

The big circular watchtower called **Ta Dzong** has been converted into the **National Museum** and is a rich source of information on Bhutanese history and culture. Among the exhibits are *thangkhas* (paintings), jewellery, household artefacts, postage stamps and weapons, and a section on natural history. Special exhibits feature periods of Bhutanese history and specialized aspects of Buddhism. The museum is open Tuesday to Saturday.

Dating from the mid 17th century, **Drugyel Dzong**, at the northern end of the valley, was a fortified monastery built to resist Tibetan invasions. It now stands in ruins, but the bustle of the surrounding villages and the horse caravans ambling through seem to transport you into a living past.

Paro is the starting point for treks to the famed Tiger's Nest, **Taktshang**, where Guru Rinpoche was believed to have landed his flying tigress when he came to Bhutan in the 8th century. By any standards, this traditional monastery is a structural feat, built against a sheer rock face around a sacred cave, where many saints and sages used to meditate. Paro Taktshang was seriously damaged by fire in 1998 but rebuilt and fully restored by the end of 2004. The strenuous walk up steep forest paths takes about two hours, and somewhat less to come down. Horses or mules are available to carry the less active most of the way.

In winter, the central monk order still resides at **Punakha**, the old capital of Bhutan, a two hours' drive east of Thimphu by way of the spectacular Dochula Pass, 3,050 m (10,000 ft). At an altitude of 1,250 m (4,100 ft), it enjoys a sub-tropical climate in an extremely fertile region. Two glacial rivers, the Phochhu (Male River) and the Mochhu (Female River), join at the centre of the valley and meander southwards through the Himalayan foothills into India. At the fork of the two rivers sits the **Punakha Dzong**, the seat of Zhabdrung Ngawang Namgyal, who unified Bhutan in the 17th century. The *dzong* has been destroyed over the years by fire and glacial floods, but Jigme Singye Wangchuck ordered its restoration and today it is a fine example of Bhutanese craftsmanship. Among other treasures, it houses the remains of Zhabdrung Ngawang Namgyal and a small image of Chenrezig, the Buddha of Compassion (Avalokiteshwara), which was believed to have created itself on a vertebra of a Buddhist saint, Choegyal Tsangpa Gyaray.

A short drive up the valley, the **Khamsum Yulley Chhorten** *(stupa)* was built in 1992 by Queen Ashi Tshering Yangdon. It is similar in architectural style to the National Memorial Chhorten in Thimphu.

South of Punakha, on the national highway, is the **Wangdue Phodrang** valley, with a majestic *dzong* overlooking the highway that forks towards the east and the south. In the same valley stands the monastery of the 15th-century lama Drukpa Kuenley, known as the Divine Madman, a popular saint who is invoked to bless couples who have difficulty conceiving.

Phobjikha valley west of the Black Mountains is the winter home of the rare Black Necked Crane that migrates from Tibet in the late autumn.

The central valley of **Trongsa** was the seat of Bhutanese leaders who preceded the monarchy, established in 1907, and of the first two kings. This narrow but starkly beautiful valley is dominated by the historic **Trongsa Dzong**. Built in 1647, it became the official seat of the Crown Prince of Bhutan preceding his ascension to the throne. It underwent major conservation work in recent years and was officially declared fully restored in 2004.

The central district of **Bumthang**, said to be the most beautiful valley in Bhutan, is the spiri-

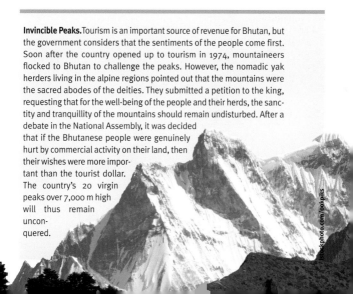

Invincible Peaks. Tourism is an important source of revenue for Bhutan, but the government considers that the sentiments of the people come first. Soon after the country opened up to tourism in 1974, mountaineers flocked to Bhutan to challenge the peaks. However, the nomadic yak herders living in the alpine regions pointed out that the mountains were the sacred abodes of the deities. They submitted a petition to the king, requesting that for the well-being of the people and their herds, the sanctity and tranquillity of the mountains should remain undisturbed. After a debate in the National Assembly, it was decided that if the Bhutanese people were genuinely hurt by commercial activity on their land, then their wishes were more important than the tourist dollar. The country's 20 virgin peaks over 7,000 m high will thus remain unconquered.

istockphoto.com/lookpiks

The mantra "om mani padme hum" inscribed on a pile of sacred stones.

tual heartland of the country, dotted with some of the most sacred and ancient monasteries and pilgrimage sites in the kingdom. Apart from the 17th-century **Jakar Dzong**, the seat of local government and the clergy at Jakar, there are about 90 monasteries in the district, and numerous local festivals are held.

At the centre of Bumthang Valley, north of Jakar, the 7th-century **Jambay Lhakhang** was built by the Tibetan king Songtsen Gam-

bo. It is best known today for a fire dance festival held in autumn.

When he established Buddhism in Bhutan, Guru Rinpoche was said to have tamed the demons plaguing Bumthang Valley. He also set up important sites, such as the **Kurje Lhakhang**, where the kings of Bhutan are cremated. At the north end of the valley, Kurje is a popular destination for all Buddhists.

Bumthang was also home to the Pema Lingpa lineage, ancestors of the Wangchuck dynasty. Pema Lingpa (1450–1521) was one of the most holy men of Bhutan, known as a "treasure hunter", whose knowledge of hidden relics came to him through dreams and visions of Guru Rinpoche. He built **Tamshing Lhakhang** monastery, which is preserved as a national treasure.

Dining Out

Looking down on towns and villages, you'll notice the bright red roofs of many houses. On closer view, it turns out to be chillis drying in the sun. In Bhutan the chilli is eaten as a vegetable. By any standard, the food is hot, the national dish being *ema datschi*, chilli cooked with cheese. Food in hotels and restaurants is toned down for foreigners but can still be a little too spicy for those not used to it. Restaurant cuisine

Gross National Happiness
Inspired by Buddhist teachings, King Jigme Singye Wangchuck declared in 1972 that his official development goal would be Gross National Happiness, interpreted as a balance between socio-economic progress, protection of the pristine environment, good governance, and the preservation of the ancient Bhutanese culture. In essence it means that, while economic development is important, real priorities should not be overlooked. The world must always bear in mind the basic human needs and values in the quest for material gain. This policy is gaining recognition today as government leaders, scholars and intellectuals attempt to clarify the unique concept.

tends to be a mixture of Bhutanese, Indian, Chinese and western food, and for group tours, buffet meals are usually provided.

The staple in much of the country is red rice, a tasty, healthy variety of medium-grain mountain rice. Part of the red bran is left on the grain which turns pale pink, soft and slightly sticky when cooked. Other regional staples are buckwheat dough and noodles in the centre, wheat in the north, and maize in the east.

Air-dried meat and dried vegetables are popular, and dried yak (similar to jerky) is a delicacy in winter and early spring.

You might like to try the food at small local restaurants, but it can be risky for delicate eaters. Open-air stalls by the roadside and small back-street places should be avoided.

Drinks

The Bhutanese are fond of alcohol and will be quick to offer a variety of drinks. Commercially produced whisky and rum are popular. Bhutan also produces brandy, gin, a number of herbal alcoholic drinks, and Red Panda beer. For a more unusual experience, try the home brews, mainly the strong colourless spirit, *ara*, sometimes served hot with a fried egg in it, and bangchang, a warm beer. Both drinks are made from a variety of grain.

There is a variety of fruit juices, and bottled water is available all over Bhutan and is carried on treks by the organizers. Local people are sometimes partial to hot boiled water, traditional salted butter tea and sweet, strong, milky tea.

Shopping

Handicrafts are generally produced for local use, but a number of shops sell woodcarvings, metal sculptures, jewellery and paintings obviously intended for visitors. However, many of these are made in Nepal, and prices are notably high. Souvenirs such as T-shirts, purses and bags, silk bookmarks and excellent postcards are available. Every district town has a vegetable market, mostly open at weekends, and each one is fun to visit; despite the name, they will also sell local handicrafts.

Bhutan's paintings are inspired by Buddhism and are rich in imagery and symbolism. These *thangkhas* are painted on canvas and the tradition is to use mineral paints, although modern artists now tend to prefer acrylic colours that give a bright new look. The paintings are usually framed in brocade silk like a scroll. It is illegal to export antiques, and old *thangkhas*, statues, masks and so on should have a seal from the shop to certify that they are not antiques. This is checked at the airport customs on departure.

Handwoven textiles in silk, cotton and wool are gaining popularity in the international market. The designs are symbolic, inspired by nature and religious traditions. You can buy lengths of fabric for the *gho* (men's coat) or *kira* (women's long skirt), or other pieces determined by the size of the loom. The eastern district of Lhuentsi is known for silk, while Bumthang produces a thick woollen weave, *yathra*. But you'll find the best choice in Thimphu.

Hand tools are used for most crafts, which makes each item unique, though the finish may be rough. Clasps, *koma*, for holding together the traditional dress, are usually made in silver and linked with chains. Betel nut boxes in silver with hand-tooled motifs are quite expensive but make attractive gifts. The wide selection of jewellery includes stones and silver beads from different regions of the Himalayas, brought from Nepal and India.

Paper is made by hand from the Daphne plant and is used for traditional gift-wrapping, for writing and printing scriptures. It is strong, and available in colours achieved with vegetable dyes, sometimes with a deckled edge. Silk threads, leaves, flower petals or even small torn pieces of banknotes can be mixed into the pulp, with unique results.

Hand-turned wooden bowls, pots and plates, or *duppas*, are made in the Trashiyangtse district in the far east of Bhutan, and reflect the skills of the craftsmen who do not use power tools. The duppa made of burlwood (tree knots) are highly prized—and more expensive.

Browse the Thimphu bookshops for interesting publications on Bhutan and Buddhism. A few books about local folk tales are available in paperback.

Cassettes or CDs feature popular or classical songs and instrumentals. The quality varies, so it's best to listen before you buy. Generally the Royal Academy for Performing Arts has a good selection of traditional music.

Bhutan's postage stamps are often highly original in shape, design and material. Special issues of the 1960s and 1970s include silk, steel, perfumed, relief or "talking" stamps (tiny vinyl records that play the national anthem or recount the country's history). In 2008 the country issued the world's first CD-Rom postage stamp. Visit the philately counter at the Thimphu and Phuentsholing post offices for a wide selection. You may also find ready-assembled albums in handicraft shops.

PRACTICAL INFORMATION

Climate. Bhutan's climate ranges dramatically from the hot tropic south that borders India to the freezing temperatures of the great northern glaciers. The inhabited central belt where visitors would normally go, however, is mild most of the year round. Rain is expected between June and August. Spring, autumn, and winter usually see clear sunny days and cold nights.

Communications. There is a good digital telecom network in Bhutan, offering clear lines and international direct dialling as well as Internet connections. There is at least one public telephone kiosk in every town. The local mobile service is available in most districts, but connections may sometimes be difficult on the winding mountain roads. It is possible to buy SIM cards for temporary use. Internet services are also available in internet cafes in almost every town.

Currency. The *Ngultrum*, divided into 100 *chhertum*, is pegged to the Indian Rupee. Banknotes: Nu. 5, 10, 50, 100, 500; coins 20, 25, 50 chetrum and Nu. 1. Indian banknotes up to 100 rupees also circulate.

Credit cards. Major credit and charge cards are accepted in a few of the shops and main hotels; mostly in the capital and Paro.

Electricity. The current is 240 V, using two or three-pin round sockets, usually 15A and 5A.

Hours. Working hours are Monday to Friday 9 a.m.–5 p.m., with a one hour lunch break.

Smoking. In 2004 Bhutan was the first country in the world to place a ban on the sale of tobacco products. You can bring in your own cigarettes but will have to pay a 200 per cent tax on arrival at the airport. Smoking is prohibited in public places.

Time difference. Bhutan follows UTC/GMT +6 (30 minutes ahead of India).

Tipping. A tip will be appreciated in hotels and restaurants, perhaps Nu. 20 or 30 for small meals or services and Nu. 50 if the service is particularly appreciated. Guides and drivers are generally tipped more.

Water. Bottled mineral water is widely available. Tap water is not safe to drink. Avoid drinking water from any flask or water container, even in restaurants, because some of the water is untreated.

General editor
Barbara Ender-Jones

English adaptation
Judith Farr
Lisa Costantini

Additional text
Dan Colwell (Rajasthan)
Don Allan (Nepal)
Siok Sian Pek (Bhutan)
Susanne Gupta (Brahmaputra)

Design
Karin Palazzolo

Layout
Luc Malherbe, Matias Jolliet

Photo credits
P. 1: Renata Holzbachová
P. 2: Eastenhuh (doorway);
istockphoto.com/Artubo (prayer
flags); Amre Ghiba (desert);
Dan.be (flowers)

Maps
JPM Publications, Mathieu Germay

Copyright © 2012, 2000
JPM Publications S.A.
12, avenue William-Fraisse,
1006 Lausanne, Switzerland
information@jpmguides.com
http://www.jpmguides.com/

Every care has been taken to
verify the information in the
guide, but the publisher cannot
accept responsibility for any
errors that may have occurred.
If you spot an inaccuracy or a
serious omission, please let
us know.

Printed in Germany
12908.00.11748
Edition 2012–2013